collections

Houghton Mifflin Harcourt

Close Reader

TEACHER'S GUIDE

GRADE 9

Program Consultants:

Kylene Beers

Martha Hougen

Carol Jago

William L. McBride

Erik Palmer

Lydia Stack

HISTORY

Cover, Title Page Photo Credits: ©Marc Guitierrez/Getty Images

Printed in the U.S.A.

ISBN 978-0-544-08800-9

4 5 6 7 8 9 10   1420   22 21 20 19 18 17 16 15 14

4500470058   B C D E F G

Close Reading— It's a Habit of Mind

By Carol Jago

You read closely every day. Each time you open a bank statement, mull over a new poem in the *New Yorker*, or grade a student paper, you perform a close reading. Often what appears on the page doesn't at first quite make sense. So what do you do? You read the text again, paying attention to places where comprehension broke down, focusing on unfamiliar words or familiar words used in unfamiliar ways. Sometimes you ask a friend for help when the meaning continues to elude you. Close reading isn't a strategy; it's a habit of mind.

In the past we protected students from texts they might find difficult, offering them only "considerate text" that made clear what the main ideas were and simplified dense passages. Unfortunately, college and career-readiness, not to mention the demands of citizenship, requires that students master the art of negotiating a great many inconsiderate texts. We thought we were helping students—trust me, no one has spent more time looking for shorter, easier, funnier things for kids to read than me—but we only succeeded in making the transition to college more difficult. The *Close Reader* offers students various protocols that, once internalized, will allow them to read independently with comprehension the complex texts called for in the Common Core State Standards.

Fortunately, many of these seemingly "inconsiderate" texts are also some of the finest literature ever written. The works of William Shakespeare, Homer, and Ralph Waldo Emerson as well as those of Isabelle Allende, Gwendolyn Brooks, and Ray Bradbury repay the investment of time and trouble taken to read them closely many times over. (So does an accurately read bank statement.)

Cognitive neuroscientist Maryanne Wolf, director of the Center for Reading and Language Research at Tufts University, warns that much of the reading today's young people are doing on the Internet develops a habit of what she calls a state of "continuous partial attention." In *Proust and the Squid: The Story and Science of the Reading Brain* (2007), Wolf describes how the time children spend daily processing a steady stream of online information is actually reshaping the architecture of their brains. As an English teacher, my concern is that while skimming and scanning may be an efficient and effective way to read a Twitter or Facebook feed, it's a very poor way to read poetry. I need my students to develop the ability to read profoundly and introspectively. And independently!

Common Core Anchor Standard #10 for reading states that students must "Read and comprehend complex literary and informational texts independently and proficiently." Working through this *Close Reader* will help your students perform proficiently by developing their independence as readers. As they practice unpacking challenging text for themselves, getting into the habit of rereading, slowing down when the going gets tough, knowing what to do when they meet a new word, students become more confident readers. We can't do the reading for them, not now or later. The *Close Reader* will give you ideas for what to do instead.

Let's make this a nation of close readers.

COLLECTION 1
Finding Common Ground

COLLECTION 2
The Struggle for Freedom

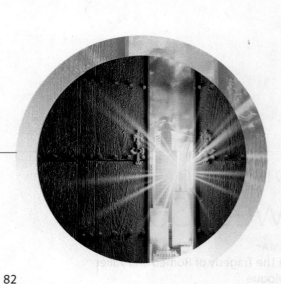

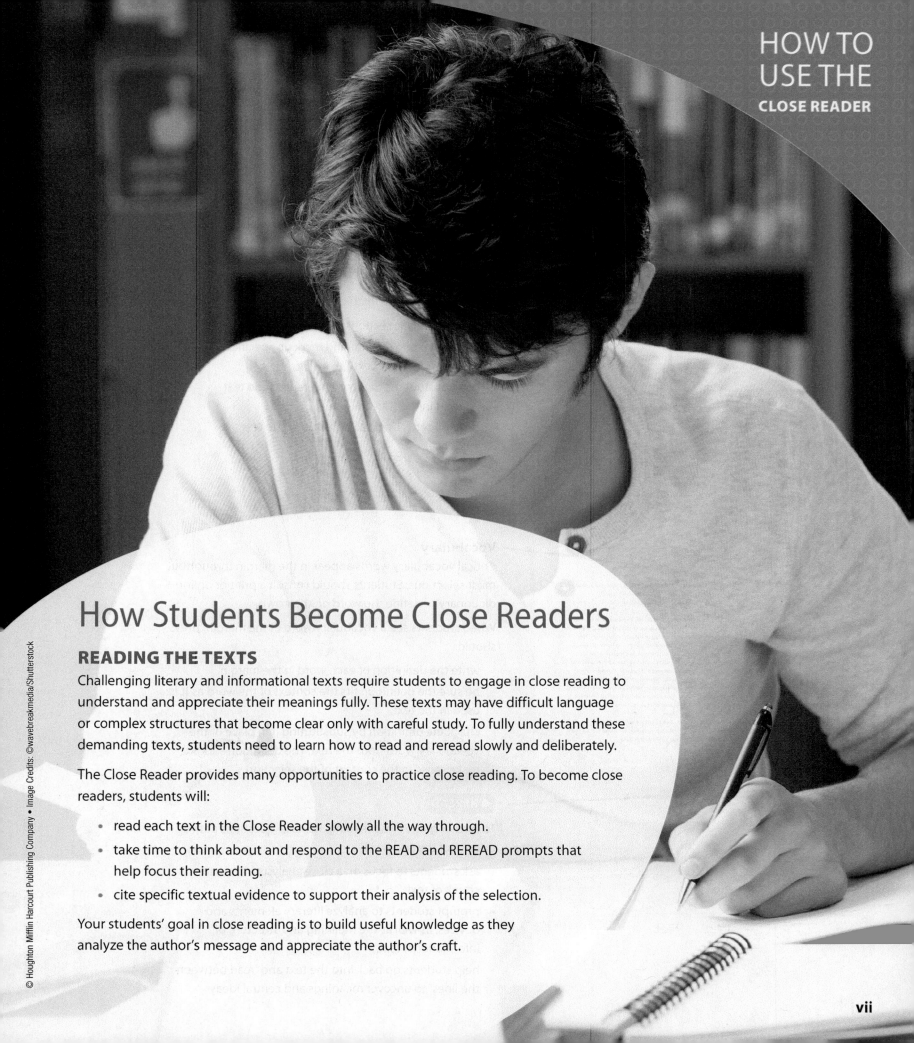

How Students Become Close Readers

READING THE TEXTS

Challenging literary and informational texts require students to engage in close reading to understand and appreciate their meanings fully. These texts may have difficult language or complex structures that become clear only with careful study. To fully understand these demanding texts, students need to learn how to read and reread slowly and deliberately.

The Close Reader provides many opportunities to practice close reading. To become close readers, students will:

- read each text in the Close Reader slowly all the way through.
- take time to think about and respond to the READ and REREAD prompts that help focus their reading.
- cite specific textual evidence to support their analysis of the selection.

Your students' goal in close reading is to build useful knowledge as they analyze the author's message and appreciate the author's craft.

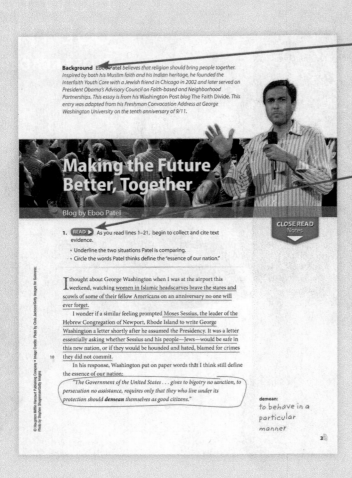

Background

This paragraph provides information about the text students are about to read. It helps them understand the context of the selection through additional information about the author, the subject, or the time period in which the text was written.

READ ▶

Questions and specific instructions at the beginning of the selection and on the bottom of the pages will guide students through a close reading of each text.

These questions and instructions:

- refer to specific sections of the text.

- ask students to look for and mark up specific information in the text.

- prompt students to record inferences and text analysis in the side margins.

- help students begin to collect and cite text evidence.

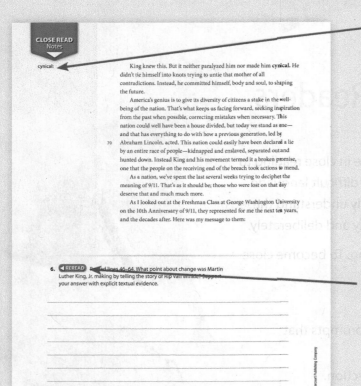

Vocabulary

Critical vocabulary words appear in the margin throughout most selections. Students should consult a print or online dictionary to define the word on their own.

When students see a vocabulary word in the margin, they should:

- write the definition of each word in the margin.

- be sure the definition fits the context of the word as **it** is used in the text.

- check the definition by substituting it in place of the vocabulary word from the text. The definition should make sense in the context of the selection.

◀ REREAD

To further guide close reading, REREAD questions at the bottom of the page will:

- ask students to focus on a close analysis of a smaller chunk of text.

- prompt students to analyze literary elements and devices, as well as the meaning and structure of informational text.

- help students go back into the text and "read between the lines" to uncover meanings and central ideas.

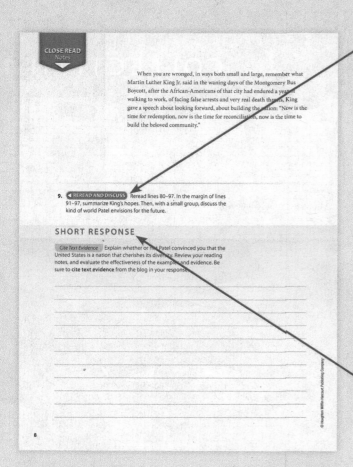

These prompts encourage students to work with a partner or in a small group to discuss specific events, details, statements, and evidence from the text. These discussions will allow students to acquire and share knowledge about the texts they are reading.

As they engage in these discussions, students should:

- be sure to cite specific text evidence in support of their statements.

- pose questions and integrate their ideas with the ideas of others.

- collaborate to reach a consensus or call attention to evidence that might have been missed or misinterpreted.

- acknowledge the views of others and be ready to modify their own thinking.

SHORT RESPONSE

At the end of each text, students will have an opportunity to sum up their thinking by completing a Short Response. The Short Response represents a place to convey some of the ideas they have developed through close reading of the text.

When students write the Short Response, they should:

- review all margin notes and REREAD responses.

- circle or highlight evidence from the notes that supports their position or point of view.

- clearly state a point of view and support it with reasons.

- cite specific text evidence to support their reasons.

Finding Common Ground

COLLECTION 1

Finding Common Ground

"We may have different religions, different languages, different colored skin, but we all belong to one human race."

—Kofi Annan

Making the Future Better, Together

Blog by Eboo Patel

Why This Text

Students may have difficulty thoroughly understanding the writer's ideas and evidence in an argument. The following argument by Eboo Patel cites complex reasoning and difficult quotations that become clear only with careful study. With the help of the close-reading questions, students will trace and evaluate Patel's argument that claims that the United States is a nation that cherishes its diversity. This close reading will guide students to comprehend Patel's argument.

Background Have students read the background and biographical information about Eboo Patel, the founder and president of the Interfaith Youth Core. That organization brings together people of all faiths to work together to build a better future. Patel has written for numerous publications and has spoken at universities around the world. His blog *The Faith Divide* examines religious issues that unite people—and issues that drive them apart.

AS YOU READ Ask students to pay close attention to the reasons Patel gives to support his position about diversity in America. How soon into Patel's blog can they begin to identify his point of view?

Common Core Support

- cite strong and thorough textual evidence
- analyze how an author's ideas or claims are developed and refined
- trace and evaluate an argument
- assess an author's claims and reasoning

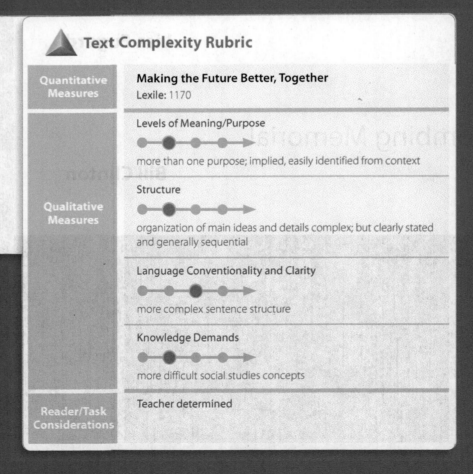

Text Complexity Rubric

Quantitative Measures

Making the Future Better, Together
Lexile: 1170

Qualitative Measures

Levels of Meaning/Purpose

more than one purpose; implied, easily identified from context

Structure

organization of main ideas and details complex; but clearly stated and generally sequential

Language Conventionality and Clarity

more complex sentence structure

Knowledge Demands

more difficult social studies concepts

Reader/Task Considerations

Teacher determined

Trace and Evaluate an Argument

Students should read this blog carefully all the way through. Close-reading questions at the bottom of the page will help them focus on a thorough analysis of the argument and the evidence, including details, facts, quotations, and examples that support them. As they read, students should record comments or questions about the text in the side margins.

WHEN STUDENTS STRUGGLE . . .

To help students follow the reasons Patel gives to support his claim about our nation's respect for diversity, have students work in a small group to fill out a chart such as the one shown below as they analyze the blog entry.

CITE TEXT EVIDENCE For practice in tracing an argument, ask students to cite the evidence Patel uses to support each reason.

CLAIM: *The United States is a nation that cherishes its diversity.*

SUPPORT:

Reason 1: *He cites George Washington's view that the nation needed to be built without bigotry or ethnic or religious persecution.*

Reason 2: *He agrees with Washington that a diverse democracy based on respect, relationship, and service to the common good will thrive.*

Reason 3: *He states that the "essence of our nation" is still that people's identities will be respected, their freedoms protected, and their safety secured.*

Reason 4: *He agrees with the idea of Dr. Martin Luther King Jr. that for real change to occur, people must work together to build bridges, community, and the future.*

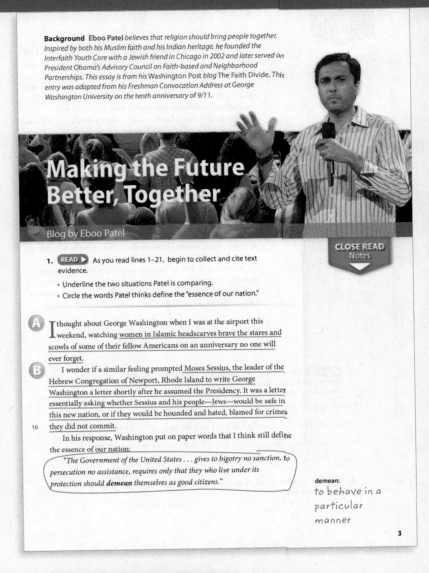

Background *Eboo Patel believes that religion should bring people together. Inspired by both his Muslim faith and his Indian heritage, he founded the Interfaith Youth Core with a Jewish friend in Chicago in 2002 and later served on President Obama's Advisory Council on Faith-based and Neighborhood Partnerships. This essay is from his Washington Post blog* The Faith Divide. *This entry was adapted from his Freshman Convocation Address at George Washington University on the tenth anniversary of 9/11.*

Making the Future Better, Together

Blog by Eboo Patel

CLOSE READ
Notes

1. **READ ▷** As you read lines 1–21, begin to collect and cite text evidence.

 • Underline the two situations Patel is comparing.
 • Circle the words Patel thinks define the "essence of our nation."

A I thought about George Washington when I was at the airport this weekend, watching women in Islamic headscarves brave the stares and scowls of some of their fellow Americans on an anniversary no one will ever forget.

B I wonder if a similar feeling prompted Moses Sessius, the leader of the Hebrew Congregation of Newport, Rhode Island to write George Washington a letter shortly after he assumed the Presidency. It was a letter essentially asking whether Sessius and his people—Jews—would be safe in this new nation, or if they would be hounded and hated, blamed for crimes 10 they did not commit.

 In his response, Washington put on paper words that I think still define the essence of our nation:

 "The Government of the United States . . . gives to bigotry no sanction, to persecution no assistance, requires only that they who live under its protection should **demean** themselves as good citizens."

demean: to behave in a particular manner

3

---

1. **READ AND CITE TEXT EVIDENCE** Explain that Patel compares two situations to open his blog—one from the present, the other from the past—prefacing the situations with a reference to George Washington to get the reader's attention.

A ASK STUDENTS to identify the two situations Patel is comparing, citing evidence from lines 1–21, and citing words and sentences from Washington that Patel thinks define the "essence of our nation." *Responses may include specific references to lines 2–4 and 5–10, and to lines 11–15 and 16–21.*

Critical Vocabulary: demean (line 15) Have students share their definitions of *demean* as Washington used it in the text cited by Patel. *Washington used it to mean "to behave in a particular manner."* Point out that *demean* is a word with multiple meanings. The same word from a different origin is more commonly used today. Ask students what this word means. *It means "to degrade."*

In this new nation, the new president was saying, people would have their identities respected, their freedoms protected, their safety secured. They would be encouraged to cultivate good relationships with fellow citizens from other backgrounds, no matter the tensions and conflicts in
20 the lands from which they came. And they would be invited—and expected—to contribute to the common good of their country.

Washington came to his views through both principle and practical experience. As the leader of the Continental Army, the first truly national institution, Washington recognized he was going to need the contributions of all willing groups in America. Back then, it was a common anti-Catholic practice to burn the Pope in effigy. Washington banned this, and other anti-Catholic insults within the Continental Army, and wrote: "At such a juncture, and in such circumstances, to be insulting their Religion, is so monstrous, as not to be suffered or excused."

30 Washington brought this ethic to his private life. When seeking a carpenter and a bricklayer for his Mount Vernon estate, he remarked: "If they are good workmen, they may be of Asia, Africa, or Europe. They may be Mohometans,[1] Jews or Christians of any Sect, or they may be Atheists." What mattered is what they could build.

Wars between clans and tribes, tension between sects and groups, prejudice directed at religion or nationality—those were the problems of past centuries. And whether you are reading the news about Somalia or Libya or Europe or Oklahoma, those are the problems of our time.

[1] **Mohometans:** another term for Muslims.

2. (C) **REREAD** Reread lines 1–21. Explain how starting his article with George Washington's views on bigotry helps establish Patel's point of view. Support your answer with explicit textual evidence.

Starting the article with a quotation from Washington helps to establish Patel's point of view that people of different faiths can work together. He uses Washington as an example of people overcoming their differences to work together.

3. **READ** As you read lines 22–45, underline the details that explain Washington's reasoning.

4

(D)
40 Washington wanted America to stand for something different: not the old idea that we are better apart, but the high hope that people from the four corners of the earth could do remarkable things together, even build a nation, and show humanity that we are better together. Respect, relationship and service to the common good—that was Washington's ethic, the three pillars on which he believed a diverse democracy would thrive.

(F) In a too-seldom read sermon called "Remaining Awake Through A Great Revolution," Martin Luther King Jr. summarized the story of Rip Van Winkle. He mentioned the details we all know—old man goes up the
(E) mountain, falls asleep for many years, grows a long beard. But King pauses
50 on one detail we might have passed over: When Rip Van Winkle went up the mountain, he passed an Inn with a picture of King George III, the English monarch. When he came down the mountain some years later, the Inn was still there, but the picture had changed: it was now of George Washington. America had gone from living under a dictator to living in a democracy.

What strikes me about King's use of George Washington as a symbol of democracy is that King's great-great grandparents could well have been owned by General Washington. The man who welcomed Jews and Catholics into the nation, the man who spoke of a government that gave bigotry no
60 sanction and persecution no assistance, he was a slaveholder.

4. (D) **REREAD** Reread lines 39–45. Explain how the author supports his opinion about Washington's view of people's freedom and identity. Support your answer with explicit textual evidence.

He notes that Washington recognized that all willing groups were needed in the fight for independence. Washington believed in "respect, relationship and service to the common good."

5. **READ** As you read lines 46–64, explain King's outlook for America in the margin.

5

---

2. **REREAD AND CITE TEXT EVIDENCE** By opening his blog with a reference to George Washington's views about bigotry, Patel grabs the reader's interest and introduces the topic and point of view he will be presenting in his blog.

(B) **ASK STUDENTS** to state Patel's point of view and to support it with Washington's intolerance of bigotry, citing specific evidence from the text. *Students should recognize that Patel's point of view is similar to Washington's in that both believe that people of different backgrounds, faiths, and ethnicities can overcome their differences and work together to contribute to "the common good."*

3. **READ AND CITE TEXT EVIDENCE**

(C) **ASK STUDENTS** to cite specific details or textual evidence that explains Washington's reasoning and views concerning America's refusal to sanction bigotry. *Students should cite specific references to lines 24–25 and 39–45.*

4. **REREAD AND CITE TEXT EVIDENCE**

(D) **ASK STUDENTS** to cite explicit textual evidence that shows how Patel supports his opinion about Washington's point of view concerning freedom and personal identity. *Students should cite explicit textual evidence from lines 39–45.*

5. **READ AND CITE TEXT EVIDENCE**

(E) **ASK STUDENTS** to read their margin notes to a partner and then write one response that best states King's outlook for the United States, citing specific textual evidence. *Students should point out that King's outlook for the nation includes putting the past behind and working together as one people toward a better future.*

FOR ELL STUDENTS Tell students that Rip Van Winkle was a fictitious character from a celebrated short story written in 1819. Rip Van Winkle slept for 20 years and saw great changes once he awoke—the American Revolution had taken place and the nation had become independent.

cynical:

scornfully
negative

King has great
hope for the
future because
so much has
changed
already.

King knew this. But it neither paralyzed him nor made him **cynical.** He didn't tie himself into knots trying to untie that mother of all contradictions. Instead, he committed himself, body and soul, to shaping the future.

America's genius is to give its diversity of citizens a stake in the well-being of the nation. That's what keeps us facing forward, seeking inspiration from the past when possible, correcting mistakes when necessary. This nation could well have been a house divided, but today we stand as one—and that has everything to do with how a previous generation, led by
70 Abraham Lincoln, acted. This nation could easily have been declared a lie by an entire race of people—kidnapped and enslaved, separated out and hunted down. Instead King and his movement termed it a broken promise, one that the people on the receiving end of the breach took actions to mend.

As a nation, we've spent the last several weeks trying to decipher the meaning of 9/11. That's as it should be; those who were lost on that day deserve that and much much more.

As I looked out at the Freshman Class at George Washington University on the 10th Anniversary of 9/11, they represented for me the next ten years, and the decades after. Here was my message to them:

6. **◄ REREAD** Reread lines 46–64. What point about change was Martin Luther King, Jr. making by telling the story of Rip Van Winkle? Support your answer with explicit textual evidence.

King tells the story of Rip Van Winkle to emphasize the extreme shift in the country that happened during Washington's time. America was now a democracy. King wants to point out that for real change to occur, people must look forward and not backward. Using Washington as an example, even though Washington was a slaveowner, shows how King was able to put the past behind him and work toward a better future.

" When you serve, you are part of the future. "

G 80 I Yes, be a part of the conversation, but more importantly, take part in action. Don't forget, the people who talk for a living talk about the people who act.

For sure, ask big questions; but also make deep commitments—to your faith or philosophy, to the nation and the world, to the earth and to each other.

Debate the meaning of the events of past decades and centuries, but above all, shape the arc of the future.

H When you serve, you are part of the future. When you dream, you are part of the future. When you build bridges that show we are better together
90 you lower the barriers that make people believe we are better apart.

Patel is asking for the freshmen to participate in meaningful discussions, to make a commitment, and to shape the future.

7. **READ ▶** As you read lines 65–87, continue to cite textual evidence.
   • Underline the claims Patel makes.
   • Circle the evidence he gives to support his claims.
   • In the margin, explain what Patel is asking the Freshman Class at George Washington University to do.

8. **READ ▶** As you read lines 88–97, underline Patel's advice for students and their futures.

6
7

---

6. **REREAD AND CITE TEXT EVIDENCE**

F **ASK STUDENTS** how Patel uses King's retelling of the story of Rip Van Winkle to make a point about change. How does Patel's use of King's retelling of the story support his own argument about working together toward change? *Students should cite explicit textual evidence from lines 56–60. Responses may include the idea that for real change to occur, people must put the past behind and look toward the future.*

Critical Vocabulary: cynical (line 61) Have students share their definitions of *cynical*. Ask volunteers to give examples of cynical behavior. *Students may suggest people thinking or expecting the worst, or expecting everyone to have a selfish motivation.*

7. **READ AND CITE TEXT EVIDENCE**

G **ASK STUDENTS** to read their margin notes to a partner and then write one response, using explicit textual evidence, that explains what Patel is asking the Freshman class at George Washington University to do on the 10th anniversary of 9/11. *Students should cite explicit textual evidence from lines 80–87, pointing to the details that state that students should participate in discussion, make commitments, and take part in action in order to shape the future together.*

8. **READ AND CITE TEXT EVIDENCE**

H **ASK STUDENTS** how Patel's advice supports his own claim that by working together, we can shape the future. *Students should cite specific textual evidence from lines 91–97. Patel believes that taking part in action and working together can help shape a positive future.*

King looks
forward to
reconciliation
and building
community.

When you are wronged, in ways both small and large, remember what Martin Luther King Jr. said in the waning days of the Montgomery Bus Boycott, after the African-Americans of that city had endured a year of walking to work, of facing false arrests and very real death threats, King gave a speech about looking forward, about building the nation: "Now is the time for redemption, now is the time for reconciliation, now is the time to build the beloved community."

9. ◀ **REREAD AND DISCUSS** Reread lines 80–97. In the margin of lines 91–97, summarize King's hopes. Then, with a small group, discuss the kind of world Patel envisions for the future.

SHORT RESPONSE

Cite Text Evidence Explain whether or not Patel convinced you that the United States is a nation that cherishes its diversity. Review your reading notes, and evaluate the effectiveness of the examples and evidence. Be sure to **cite text evidence** from the blog in your response.

Responses may vary but students should explain that Eboo Patel gives examples from both George Washington and Martin Luther King Jr. to support his view of the U.S. He quotes Washington as saying, ". . . the United States . . . gives to bigotry no sanction, to persecution no assistance . . ." And he notes that Washington understood that he needed contributions from all willing groups in America. He explains that Martin Luther King Jr. was willing to use Washington, a slaveholder, as a symbol of democracy, and that King was committed to mending the past and shaping the future.

8

---

9. ▸ REREAD AND DISCUSS USING TEXT EVIDENCE

ⓘ **ASK STUDENTS** to appoint a reporter for each group to cite specific textual evidence and line numbers to support their discussion of Patel's vision for the future. *Students should cite explicit textual evidence from lines 80–90.*

SHORT RESPONSE

Cite Text Evidence Student responses will vary, but students should cite specific examples and evidence from the text to support their positions. Students should:

- explain whether or not they were convinced by Patel's argument.
- give reasons for their position on Patel's claim.
- cite specific evidence from the text to support their reasons.

TO CHALLENGE STUDENTS . . .

For more context about Patel's blog entry, students should read Dr. Martin Luther King Jr.'s complete address in which he talked about Rip Van Winkle. It is the Commencement Address for Oberlin College from 1965, entitled "Remaining Awake Through a Great Revolution," and it can be found online.

ASK STUDENTS to read King's commencement address and to reread Patel's blog entry. Encourage students to work in small groups to write an essay or blog entry that compares and contrasts King's address with Patel's advice in "Making the Future Better, Together." With the class, discuss the elements of writing a compare-and-contrast essay or blog, eliciting these points:

- Prepare one list of your subjects' similarities and another list of their differences.
- Write your central idea in a sentence that clearly states what you are comparing and contrasting.
- Write supporting sentences that include details, facts, examples, and quotations to explain how the two subjects are alike and different.
- Use words and phrases to show similarities, such as *similarly, like, in the same way,* and others to show differences, such as *unlike, however, but,* and *on the contrary.*
- Organize your writing in one of two ways: by presenting one paragraph about similarities and another about differences, or by describing the key characteristics of your first subject in one paragraph and then the key characteristics of your second subject in another paragraph. As you describe the second subject, point out similarities and differences with the first subject.

Have group members plan, write, revise, and proofread their essay or blog, publishing and sharing their essay with the class or posting their blog for everyone to read.

DIG DEEPER

With the class, return to Question 9, Reread and Discuss. Have students share their summaries about the hopes expressed by Dr. Martin Luther King Jr. Then have them share the results of their group discussion about the kind of world Eboo Patel envisions for the future.

ASK STUDENTS whether they were satisfied with their summaries of King's hopes and with the outcome of their small-group discussions. Have each group share what they saw as Patel's vision for the future. Did they agree or disagree with his vision? What convincing evidence did the groups cite from Patel's blog to support this opinion?

- Guide students to assess their summaries by checking to see that they include only the most important facts, details, and examples concerning Dr. King's hopes.
- Encourage groups to tell whether there was any compelling evidence cited by group members holding a different view of Patel's vision for the world of the future. Ask why the textual evidence cited wasn't strong enough to sway the group's position.
- Have groups explain how they determined whether or not they had found sufficient evidence to support what they saw as Patel's vision for the future. Did everyone in the group agree as to what made the evidence sufficient? How did the group resolve any conflicts or disagreements?
- After students have shared the results of their group's discussion, ask whether another group shared any ideas they wish they had considered.

ASK STUDENTS to return to their Short Response answer to revise it based on the class discussion concerning Patel's vision for the future.

CLOSE READING NOTES

Night Calls

Short Story by Lisa Fugard

Why This Text

Students sometimes find it difficult to infer the theme of a story. "Night Calls" provides an opportunity to analyze character development and interpret symbols in order to determine the story's theme. With the help of the close-reading questions, students will support their inferences about the characters with textual evidence. This close reading will lead students to determine the theme of "Night Calls."

Background Have students read the background and the information about the author. "Night Calls" develops the central idea of a daughter's yearning to connect with a distant father. Introduce the selection by telling students that Lisa Fugard grew up in South Africa, where the story is set. Tell students to be on the lookout for a key event we learn in a flashback near the start of the story.

AS YOU READ Ask students to pay attention to clues to the story's theme: its underlying message. Remind them to look for clues to the theme in what the text says explicitly and to draw inferences about the theme based on the text.

 COMMON CORE
Common Core Support

- cite strong and thorough textual evidence
- determine a theme or central idea of a text
- analyze how complex characters develop over the course of a text
- determine the meaning of words and phrases as they are used in the text

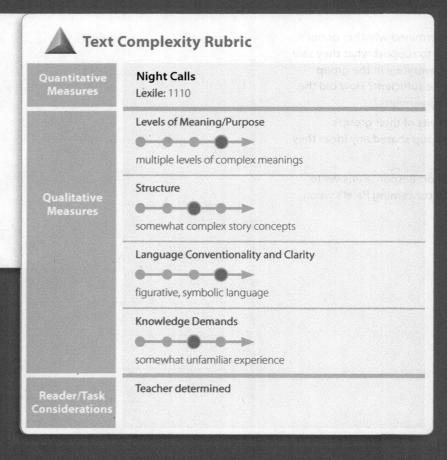

Text Complexity Rubric

Quantitative Measures

Night Calls
Lexile: 1110

Qualitative Measures

Levels of Meaning/Purpose

multiple levels of complex meanings

Structure

somewhat complex story concepts

Language Conventionality and Clarity

figurative, symbolic language

Knowledge Demands

somewhat unfamiliar experience

Reader/Task Considerations

Teacher determined

Strategies for CLOSE READING

Support Inferences About Theme

Students should read this story carefully all the way through. Close-reading questions at the bottom of the page will help them focus on a thorough analysis of the story. As they read, students should jot down comments or questions about the text in the side margins.

WHEN STUDENTS STRUGGLE . . .

To help students make and support inferences about the theme, have them work in a small group to fill out a chart, such as the one shown below, as they analyze the story.

CITE TEXT EVIDENCE For practice in supporting inferences about the theme of "Night Calls," ask students to cite evidence from the text to support their answers to the questions about Marlene, her father, and the heron.

	TEXTUAL EVIDENCE
What does Marlene want at the beginning of the story?	*She wants to be close to her father. She offers to do bird calls at night at the foot of his bed.*
What is Marlene's father like at the beginning of the story?	*Marlene's father is distant. He is neglecting his work and his daughter.*
How does the father's life change when the heron comes to the sanctuary?	*The heron gives the father hope after he loses his wife. He shares news about the heron with Marlene.*
How does the relationship between Marlene and her father change after the heron is freed?	*After the heron is free, the father feels hopeful again. Father and daughter grow closer. They work together making repairs to the compound.*
Why does Marlene imitate the heron's call at the end of the story?	*Marlene wants to protect her father's feelings. She has been trying to reach out to him throughout the whole story.*

Inferred Theme: *Giving and receiving love can be challenging.*

Background *Lisa Fugard grew up in South Africa, the daughter of the playwright and actor Athol Fugard and Sheila Fugard, a novelist and poet. Fugard came to the United States in 1980 and worked as an actress before she turned to writing. The following story is set in South Africa, though the red-crested heron Fugard describes does not actually exist.*

Night Calls

Short Story by Lisa Fugard

CLOSE READ
Notes

1. **READ ▶** As you read lines 1–26, begin to collect and cite text evidence.

   • Underline text that describes the narrator's father.
   • Circle text that hints at the narrator's feelings toward her father.

My father's hands were huge. Slablike. When he was idle, they seemed to hang off the ends of his arms like two chunks of meat. He sat on his hands during the months he courted my mother.

When I was thirteen, I watched my thin hand disappear into his. It was at the train station at Modder River. I'd come home for the September holidays. It was hot, and the only other car at the small station pulled away. The siding at Modder River, 150 miles north of Johannesburg, was never busy. I remember it all clearly, standing in the dust, watching him get out of the truck and walk toward me, noticing that there was no smile on his face but still feeling my body move toward him, my arms opening for an embrace, something rising in my throat. My father stopped and held out his right hand.

Once in the truck, I was filled with anxiety about how close to him I could sit. I settled in the middle of my half of the bench seat and watched his large, brown hand move from the steering wheel to the gearshift and back. I breathed deeply. Suddenly I was filled with the smell of him:

Ⓐ 10 **Ⓑ**

The narrator wants a hug from her father, but instead she gets a handshake.

9

---

1. **READ AND CITE TEXT EVIDENCE** Point out to students that the narrator's descriptions of her father and of herself help establish the characters and their interactions.

Ⓐ ASK STUDENTS to find text that gives hints about how the narrator feels toward her father. *Students should notice that the narrator wants his affection (lines 10–11) and she is nervous in his company (line 13). These feelings are mirrored in line 18 ("I felt like a thief") and in line 25 ("Laughingly, I turned to find my father's smile").*

FOR ELL STUDENTS Clarify the multiple meanings of the noun *calls*. Ask volunteers to provide the meaning they already probably know. Then explain that in the context of this selection, *calls* means "cries that animals make to alert others."

She wants
his approval
for her guinea
fowl call,
but he does
not respond.

Borkum Riff tobacco, sweat, the sweet odor of cheap Cape brandy. Filled with his secrets, I felt like a thief and moved a little closer to the window.

Then we were at the entrance to the Modder River Wildlife Sanctuary, and I jumped out of the car to open the gate. It swung easily, once I unlatched it, and banged against the wooden fence post, startling several guinea fowl that scampered into the veld.[1] "Krrdll . . . krrdll . . . krrdll," I called, and they slowed down. I mimicked their rattling cry again, and they stopped. Again, and a few of them stepped hesitantly toward me. Laughingly, I turned to find my father's smile, but his face was gone, blotted out by the expanse of blue sky reflected in the windshield.

C I have a gift for mimicking bird and animal calls. During my third year at boarding school I'd finally made myself popular and gained the respect of Wendy Venter, the bully of our dorm, by doing several calls late one night. It became a ritual, and every couple of weeks, around midnight, I'd hear rustling and whispering from the eleven other girls in the dormitory; then a balled-up sock would land on my bed, usually right next to my head, and Wendy would call my name in a sly whisper, "Marlene." The dorm would fall silent. Lying back in the darkness I'd start with the deep moan of the spotted eagle owl; then the high-pitched yip of the black-backed jackal; the low snuffle and violent laugh of the hyena; and then a deadly combination: the rasping, half-swallowed growl of the leopard, followed by the wild scream of the chacma baboon. Inevitably one of the younger girls would begin to cry, and I'd hear Wendy snickering in the darkness.

The narrator
probably felt
disappointed
and rejected.

D I'd told my father about this during my next trip home, about how much the other girls had enjoyed it, and I offered to do it for him one evening, offered to steal into his room at midnight, crouch at the foot of his bed, and make the calls for him. He'd shaken his head ever so slightly. "I've got the real thing right outside my window," he said.

E As we drove up to our house now, I noticed the shabby state of the compound. The road was rutted and washed-out in many places by the spring rains. The visitors' kiosk was boarded up, and the map of the sanctuary had been knocked off its post and lay on the ground. Even the

---

[1] **veld:** in South Africa, open grassy country with few bushes and almost no trees.

---

2. ◀ REREAD   Reread lines 4–12 and lines 19–26. In the margins, explain what the narrator wants from her father and what she gets instead.

3. READ ▶   As you read lines 27–44, continue to cite textual evidence.
- Circle the reason why the narrator describes her ability to mimic bird and animal calls "a gift."
- Underline her father's response to her calls.

10

---

pond had been neglected. When my parents had first come to Modder River, five years before I was born, my father had had the pond dug out for my mother. An avid botanist,[2] she'd planted it with indigenous water lilies that she collected, along with bulrushes, seven-weeks ferns, and floating hearts. During the two years when the Modder River was reduced to a trickle by the drought, the local farmers had been astonished to hear that my father was actually pumping precious water from our borehole into the pond to prevent it from drying up. An **opulent** jewel in the dusty, cracked landscape, it became a haven for birds, being visited by pied kingfishers, mountain chats, spoonbills, bokmakieries, a pair of black-shouldered kites—all told, my mother counted 107 different species. Now a thick layer of brown scum covered the shallow, stagnant water. I remembered a letter that I'd received from my father several months before. The scrawled handwriting hadn't even looked like his. I'd read it once and then hidden it away, scared by the loneliness that the words hinted at.

None of this seemed to matter, however, when I stood among our dogs, being pelted with paws and tails and long pink tongues: King, with his tail plumed like an ostrich feather, and Blitz, a lean, black shadow. They clattered behind me as I went into my bedroom. The room was still and dark and smelled musty. Quickly I opened the wooden shutters. I moved to the chest of drawers and found the large framed photograph of my mother, frozen at age thirty-two. She was laughing, and her head was turned slightly as a lock of hair blew across her face. I traced her jaw line with my finger and moved to the mirror with the photograph, but the dogs were demanding, barking and pawing at my legs.

I ran outside with them and chased them up and down the cool stone lengths of the veranda, flying past the living room and the dining room, screeching past my father's study and back again with the dogs racing behind me. Back and forth I went, until the force of motion made me round the corner past my parents' old bedroom. I stopped, panting, trying to catch my breath. I stared at the large fenced-in area under the blue gum tree. It

opulent:
having or
showing great
wealth or
value

---

[2] **botanist:** a scientist who studies plant life.

---

4. ◀ REREAD   Reread lines 27–44. In the margin, make an inference about how the narrator probably felt about her father's response to her new talent.

5. READ ▶   As you read lines 45–94, underline details that describe how the compound at Modder River has changed. Circle words that describe changes in Marlene's father.

11

---

2. **REREAD AND CITE TEXT EVIDENCE**   Students have noted that the narrator is nervous around her father, and that she seeks his affection.

B **ASK STUDENTS** to cite evidence that shows that the narrator is probably disappointed by her father's actions. *Students should cite text in lines 9–12, where the narrator wants a hug but gets a handshake, and lines 25–26, where she expects approval for her birdcall but is ignored.*

3. **READ AND CITE TEXT EVIDENCE**

C **ASK STUDENTS** to explain in their own words why the narrator considers her ability to mimic animals a gift. Point out that she is in boarding school, and have students focus on the words *finally, respect,* and *bully* in lines 28–29 to give more context to the narrator's appreciation of her gift.

4. **REREAD AND CITE TEXT EVIDENCE**

D **ASK STUDENTS** to cite textual evidence to support their inferences about the narrator's feelings. *Students may cite the text that shows how proud the narrator is of her talent, and how she wants to share it with her father. His reaction—implying that her ability is worthless—would make the narrator feel rejected.*

5. **READ AND CITE TEXT EVIDENCE**

E **ASK STUDENTS** to compare the changes in the compound with the changes in Marlene's father, using the text evidence they have identified. *Students will probably note that both the compound and Marlene's father have deteriorated.*

Critical Vocabulary: opulent (line 56) Have students compare definitions for *opulent* and then explain the antonyms *opulent* and *shabby* (line 45) in the context of the story.

Marlene's mother died in a car crash. Marlene was sent to boarding school. Her father was ready to resign.

80 was where my father kept the red-crested night heron, one of the last of its kind.

F The year that the park officials brought the bird to Modder River had been a difficult one. My mother was killed in a car accident just before my eighth birthday. Numbly, I watched my father make funeral arrangements with the help of his sister, Annette, who drove up from Johannesburg. She was adamant: There was no way I could stay at Modder River. It was too remote, and there was my schooling to consider; my mother had been my tutor. As for my father, it made no sense for him to remain, grieving, in a place so closely associated with his wife. My father was on the verge of 90 resigning as warden of the small sanctuary when park officials telephoned about the bird. The red-crested night heron had been captured at the vlei³ on Nie Te Ver, the farm abutting the sanctuary's eastern border, and the National Parks Board wanted the heron kept at Modder River on the slim chance that they might find a mate for it.

A Mr. Vanjaarsveld arrived with the bird. "We had to tie the bugger's beak up, otherwise he'd have cut us to ribbons," he said, as he placed a large burlap bag in the pen that my father had hastily constructed. He opened the bag and then quickly stepped out and shut the gate. A few moments of silence—then a wild flurry of wings, the sound of the air being thumped, 100 and the heron hit the wire at the top of the pen and came crashing down. Again and again, till the bird lay in the dust exhausted, its wings useless. Quietly my father opened the gate and stepped inside the pen. For several minutes he squatted on his haunches in the corner and then slowly he inched his way toward the bird. Kneeling alongside it, he checked the feathers for damage, spreading the wings on the ground in front of him, like a fan. Then, making soft noises in the back of his throat, he untied the strip **G** of burlap around the heron's beak. My father stayed on at Modder River, and arrangements were made for me to go to boarding school.

³ **vlei:** in South Africa, a temporary lake formed in a marshy area during the rainy season.

---

6. **◄ REREAD** Reread lines 82–94. The narrator describes the year as "difficult." In the margin, explain in your own words what happened.

7. **READ ►** As you read lines 95–139, continue to cite textual evidence.
   • Underline the changes the heron brought to Modder River.
   • Circle text that describes the heron and its surroundings.

12

Then, making soft noises in the back of his throat, he untied the strip of burlap around the heron's beak. ❞❞

H During holidays I came home, and my father would share the latest 110 news about the heron with me. He showed me articles from the local papers lauding the conservation efforts surrounding the bird, as well as articles from foreign countries in languages we couldn't understand. He showed me the stamp that the South African government issued—a thirty-seven-cent stamp with the heron's lean profile and brilliant crest. And once he gave me a feather, a long, steel-gray feather from the tip of the heron's wing, a flight feather, and it was smooth as I stroked it against my cheek during the overnight train ride back to boarding school. But after two or three years, interest in the heron faded. The articles died down, and in private the National Parks Board expressed their doubts to my father that they would 120 ever find a mate for the bird. The sanctuary was small, and apart from a secretive leopard we didn't have any of the Big Five—animals like elephants and lions that attracted tourists. Modder River returned to the way it used to be, a trickle of visitors on the occasional weekend.

I stared at the pen for a long time now. I knew what was in there. A large gray bird, with ugly hooked feet, a long slithery neck that gave me nightmares, and a red crest that was raised during the courtship ritual. I had never seen the crest, but once I'd caught a glimpse of a small red feather that had escaped from the heron's crown. There was no need to walk

lauding: praising

The heron might symbolize hope for the father and the sanctuary.

---

8. **◄ REREAD** Reread lines 109–136. In the margin, explain what the heron might symbolize.

13

---

6. **REREAD AND CITE TEXT EVIDENCE** Students may have already inferred that Marlene's mother had died. (Her photograph showed her "frozen at age thirty-two.")

   F **ASK STUDENTS** to note Marlene's mother's death and other events mentioned in lines 82–94 that contributed to the year being "difficult" and to summarize the events in the margin.

7. **READ AND CITE TEXT EVIDENCE** The narrator has explained why the year was difficult, and that her father was ready to resign.

   G **ASK STUDENTS** to underline the changes that happen after the heron is brought to Modder River. *Students should cite specific evidence about Marlene's father deciding to stay at the sanctuary (lines 107–108) and his interest in the attention the bird brought (lines 109–113).*

8. **REREAD AND CITE TEXT EVIDENCE** Remind students that writers often develop themes through the use of symbols.

   H **ASK STUDENTS** to read their margin notes to a partner, discuss the heron as a symbol, and revise their margin notes citing text evidence. *Students may conclude that the heron is a symbol of hope, citing evidence from lines 109–116.*

Critical Vocabulary: lauding (line 111) Have students compare their definitions. Point out that a more common word from the same root is *laudable*, meaning "praiseworthy."

through the (dust) to look at the bird under the swaying blue gum tree
130 branches. I went anyway. Effortlessly, I climbed the blue gum tree, but now
it was difficult for me to squeeze into the small fork halfway up. The heron
pecked listlessly at a dried-out fish, and I noticed that the pen hadn't been
cleaned in quite a while. I'd spent many school holidays in the tree watching
my father as he fed the bird, collected the feathers during the molt,[4] and
proudly chatted with visitors. Maybe he'd known that I was up there
all the time.

I shivered. The sun had set, taking all the warmth with it, and a thin
veil of light pressed against our house and the Modder River as it crawled
like a fat brown snake out of the mountains.

140 Walking back down the length of the veranda, I peered through the
windows of the rooms we'd stopped using, the dining room with its yellow
wood table, the living room where my mother's desk was still piled high
with the field guides and books she'd used to identify unknown plants she'd
come across. The outside light flickered on, and I found my father in the
kitchen, heating up a tin of curry. We ate our dinner in silence, and then he
read a book and listened to the radio. I felt uncomfortable in the house
and longed for the morning, when I could go racing through the veld with
the dogs, go out looking for tracks and walk far into the sanctuary. At
10 P.M., as was custom, my father switched off the electricity generator and
150 went to his study, where he slept.

The low hum now gone, I lay in bed and let the night overtake me,
hungrily following the calls in the darkness. A jackal marking his territory,
the rhythmic eruptions of spring bullfrogs, the steady breath of King at the
foot of my bed. And then I heard another familiar sound, the creaking of
the gate on the heron's pen. Gently I felt my way down the hall and into my
parents' old bedroom. I hid behind the soft lace curtains, and as my eyes
grew accustomed to the night, I saw my father move slowly across the
compound carrying the heron gently under his arm, its long legs dangling
at his side. The heron's neck was liquid in the moonlight, curving and
160 swaying, at times seeming to entwine my father. Its beak glinted like a

It has been
five years, and
Marlene's
father has not
moved his
dead wife's
books from
her desk.

9. **READ ▶** As you read lines 140–179, underline language that
describes how the father seems to be changing. Make notes in the
margin in lines 140–150 about what hasn't changed.

---

dagger. One of my father's hands followed the bird's neck, lightly touching it
at times, while the other was sunk deep into the heron's soft breast, pale
gray feathers around his wrist. My father slipped by with the heron, and I
went back to bed and stared into the darkness. Later on I heard a **tremulous**
wail repeated several times. It came from the river. I knew it was the
red-crested night heron, even though I'd never heard its call before, and I
thought about my father in the darkness on the banks of the Modder River
with the bird.

At breakfast the next morning, my father told me that a hyena had
170 gotten the best of us, had finally broken into the heron's pen, because the
bird had disappeared. Under the blue gum tree we examined a huge hole in
the fence. "Yes, I think so, Dad," I said, and nodded in agreement as we
watched King and Blitz sniff inside the pen. He seemed lighter and chatted
with me about school as I helped him dismantle the fence. "Hyena," he had
said with such authority. He told me that now he might even be able to
come to the end-of-the-year recital at my school. That night I made fried
bananas and ice cream for dessert, and we listened to a radio play together.
At ten, just before he switched off the generator, I looked in the mirror and
thought, I have his eyes.

180 In bed, in the blackness, I listened to the night again. The jackal that
had been barking the previous night had moved on, and it seemed quiet out
there. It wasn't long before I heard the heron calling. I knew my father heard
it as well, and I tried to picture him in his bed. I wondered if his heart beat
like mine, an urgent knocking in my chest. I rolled over and thought of the
red-crested night heron, alone by the river, the last of its kind, and I
imagined that its crest was raised and that it picked its way delicately
through the muddy water, lifting its feet up like wet handkerchiefs.

The following night I heard the heron's call again, and I also heard
footsteps leaving our house. I knew it was my father going down to the
190 river. For ten nights the heron called and my father followed. During the
days we worked on repairing things around the compound. We cleaned up
the pond and made a day trip to the western corner of the sanctuary, where
the Modder River dropped abruptly into a densely forested ravine—gnarled
trees hung with a thick gray moss that I called "old man's beard." We

tremulous:

shaky, fearful,
or nervous

Marlene's
father seems
more engaged.
They are doing
more things
together.

10. **READ ▶** As you read lines 180–205, circle the unfolding events.

---

9. **READ AND CITE TEXT EVIDENCE**

I ASK STUDENTS to compare their notes about what has not
changed (the mother's books are still on her desk). Have students
figure out how long the books must have been there. *Students
should find that the books have been there at least five years, citing
evidence from lines 4 and 83–84, showing that the mother died just
before Marlene was eight; she is now thirteen.*

10. **READ AND CITE TEXT EVIDENCE** Marlene's father has secretly
released the heron, and his mood has changed for the better.

J ASK STUDENTS to summarize what happens in lines
180–205, and to discuss with a partner what they think the father
is doing as he leaves the house. *The father is keeping track of the
heron and making sure that it is all right.*

Critical Vocabulary: tremulous (line 164) Ask volunteers to
read their definitions. Have students discuss why the narrator
uses the phrase *tremulous wail* to refer to the heron's call.
*Students may suggest that the phrase sounds sad, or foreshadows
danger for the heron.*

collected water lilies from the dappled pools, wrapping their roots in damp newspaper and placing them in our packs. Baboons barked from the rocky ledges. We saw the spoor of the leopard, two pugmarks[5] in the rich black mud. For the drive home I sat in the back of the truck. As my father shifted to low gear and negotiated the sandy part of the road that ran alongside the river, I scanned the banks, hoping to catch a glimpse of the heron roosting, waiting for nightfall. I spent a day repairing the signs along the Succulent Trail, a one-mile loop that wound through an area that my father had filled with rare plants—aloe albida, aloe monotropa, a lydenberg cycad. We put the map back on its post and touched it up with small pots of paint, the Modder River a blue vein in the brown landscape.

Then, one long night, I didn't hear the heron's call. The bird had disappeared, and when I got out of bed the next morning, I saw that (my) (father's eyes had gone dull like a dead animal's.) I knew why but couldn't say anything. Then (he started walking all the time,) often coming home only for an hour or two in the early dawn. I'd hear the creak of the floorboards near the kitchen and the thud of Blitz's tail on the floor. I'd hear my father pacing, and then, eventually, stillness. He's lying on the sofa in his study, he's asleep now, I'd say to myself. Then the pacing again and the soft slam of the screen door. From the blue gum tree I'd see him crisscrossing the veld, like a rabid dog, always coming back to touch the river. Straining my eyes, I'd watch him walk (farther and farther away,) until he vanished into the landscape.

> [5] **spoor … pugmarks:** *Spoor* is the track or trail of a wild animal. *Pugmarks* are the footprints or trail of an animal.

The bird might symbolize hope to the father: it's the only thing he cares about since his wife died.

11. ◀ REREAD Reread lines 169–205. In the margin, explain how Marlene's relationship with her father has changed. What is her father doing at night? Support your answer with explicit textual evidence.

Marlene's father is looking for the bird who has gone missing. He said a hyena "had finally broken into the heron's pen."

12. READ ▶ As you read lines 206–231, continue to cite textual evidence.

- Circle language that describes the father in lines 206–217.
- In the margin, make an inference about what the bird might mean to the father.

Accidentally, I found the heron's remains. I was out late one afternoon, looking for a snakeskin for my next school biology project. I had chosen a rocky area, where I'd seen cobras and puff adders sunning themselves, and as I moved slowly through it, poking into crevices with a stick, I came across a broken fan of bloodied feathers. The steel-gray patina was unmistakable, and I knew it was part of the heron's wing. I scratched out a hole with my stick and buried the feathers, pushing a large rock over the small grave.

I made sandwiches for supper that night. I made extra ones for my father, but he didn't come home. I sat on the veranda with King and Blitz until ten o'clock, when I switched off the generator. Swiftly, silently, I

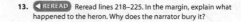

The heron was probably killed by snakes. Marlene doesn't want her father to find the bird; she knows he will be devastated.

13. ◀ REREAD Reread lines 218–225. In the margin, explain what happened to the heron. Why does the narrator bury it?

16

17

11. REREAD AND CITE TEXT EVIDENCE

Ⓚ **ASK STUDENTS** to compare their responses about Marlene's relationship with her father. *Students should see that Marlene and her father are now doing things together and are cleaning up the sanctuary.* Ask what the father does at night, and what it may have to do with his changed mood. *Students should cite evidence from lines 188–190 to explain that the father follows the heron at night. They may see some connection between the bird's freedom from the pen and the father's freedom from his despair.*

12. READ AND CITE TEXT EVIDENCE

Ⓛ **ASK STUDENTS** to describe the father's behavior that they have circled in lines 206–231. How does it compare to his behavior when he was able to hear the heron's call? Have students write what the bird might mean to the father. *Students may think that the heron symbolizes hope to the father; he rejoices in its (and his) freedom, and he is troubled by its disappearance.*

13. REREAD AND CITE TEXT EVIDENCE Marlene has been paying close attention to her father's behavior since the heron has gone.

Ⓜ **ASK STUDENTS** to cite evidence that lets them know that the heron has died. *In line 218, the narrator says that she finds the heron's remains. In the same paragraph, she recognizes the bloodied feathers of the heron.*

FOR ELL STUDENTS Point out that in South Africa—where the story is set—the English that is spoken has been influenced by the British. The use of "supper" here is equivalent to "dinner" in American English.

followed the footpath down to the far bank of the river, pushing my way
230   through the warm water that came up to my waist. I hid in the reeds and
waited.

An hour later I saw my father on the opposite bank, looking, listening.
He sat down on the dark sand and rolled a pebble in his large palms. I
 crouched even lower. Slowly I tilted my head back until my throat was wide
open and a tremulous wail slid out. My father stood up and looked across
the water to where I was crouched. Again I made the sound, again and
again. He took three more small steps toward my side of the river and his
hands fluttered like giant, tawny moths in the moonlight.

---

14.   **READ ▶**   Read lines 232–238. Underline text describing Marlene's
action and her father's response. What does she do, and why? Support
your answer with explicit textual evidence.

Marlene imitates the heron's call with the intention of making her
father think it is still alive. She wants to give him hope that the
heron is still out there.

SHORT RESPONSE

Cite Text Evidence   Think about Marlene's relationship with her father
and what it reveals about the story's theme. Review your reading notes. Be
sure to **cite text evidence** to explain your response.

At the beginning of the story, Marlene returns home and hopes for a
close relationship with her father. However, he remains distant and
seems to connect only with the heron. As Marlene begins to work
with her father fixing up the compound, he starts to warm up, but
when the bird goes missing he retreats into himself again. By the end
of the story, Marlene and her father have switched roles—she is
taking care of him. The theme of the story is about the challenges
of giving and receiving love.

18

TO CHALLENGE STUDENTS . . .

Remind students that writers often use symbols to develop their
themes. In "Night Calls," Lisa Fugard uses the red-crested heron
as a symbol of hope for the father. Have students research how
certain birds have been used as symbols in the past, and how
they are used today. For example, people think of owls as symbols
of wisdom, but in the past, writers such as William Shakespeare
used them as symbols of impending death. The dove has been
almost universally considered a symbol of peace since ancient
Egyptian times.

ASK STUDENTS to research birds as symbols in mythology,
cultures, or literature. Each student should find out about at least
one bird. Have students share the results of their research with
the class, and discuss how several of the birds might be used as
symbols in a short story.

---

14. READ AND CITE TEXT EVIDENCE

  ASK STUDENTS to find the text that describes what
Marlene does and how her father reacts. Have them explain
Marlene's action. *Marlene uses her ability as a mimic to imitate the*
heron call, knowing that her father desperately hopes that the heron
is still alive (lines 233–236). She feeds his hope.

SHORT RESPONSE

Cite Text Evidence   Student responses will vary, but they should
cite evidence from the text to support their inferences. Students
should:

- provide text-based insights into the relationship between Marlene
  and her father.
- focus on details of their relationship that develop the theme.
- determine a theme of the story that is supported by the
  relationship details.

DIG DEEPER

1. With the class, return to Question 8, Reread. Have students share their responses.

   ASK STUDENTS to cite the text evidence that led to their inferences about what the heron might symbolize.

   - Point out that lines 109–136 provide details about an earlier time, before Marlene's trip home at age thirteen. Ask students how the compound has changed since then. *The compound has not been well maintained. It is looking shabby and the pond is stagnant.*

   - Have students cite text that shows that the father was energized by the heron's presence. *He showed Marlene articles about the bird and a stamp with the heron on it.*

   - Have students cite text that shows that things changed. *The interest in the heron faded, and there were fewer visitors to the sanctuary.*

   - Have students compare the father's behavior—and the condition of the compound—when the heron first arrived and in the present setting. *Students may point out that her father was happier earlier, chatting proudly about the bird to visitors, but has now lost interest.*

   - Ask students what the heron might have meant to the father when it first lived at the sanctuary. *Students may consider the heron to be symbol of hope for the future.*

2. With the class, return to Question 11, Reread. Have students share their responses.

   ASK STUDENTS to discuss how the father acts after he releases the heron. Remind them to cite textual evidence in their discussion.

   - What clues let you know that the father is happier? *He chats with Marlene, suggests visiting her at school, and listens to the radio with her.*

   - What does the father do at night, and during the day? *He follows the bird at night. During the day he works with Marlene and seems much happier.*

   - Ask students how the heron being a symbol of hope might account for the father's behavior. *The father is happy to have set the heron free. He has also set free his own sadness, but he still somehow depends on the heron's existence.*

   ASK STUDENTS to return to their Short Response answer and revise it based on the class discussion.

CLOSE READING NOTES

Oklahoma Bombing Memorial Address

Speech by Bill Clinton

Why This Text

Readers of the text of a speech may not have the same reactions as those who hear the speech. A good speaker can advance the purpose of a speech effectively—but the words of a good speech can stand on their own. With the help of the close-reading questions, students will analyze the purpose and effectiveness of Clinton's "Oklahoma Bombing Memorial Address." This close reading will lead students to understand the purpose, rhetoric, and themes of the speech.

Background Have students read the background information about Bill Clinton and the Oklahoma City bombing. Many of the people who worked at the Alfred P. Murrah Federal Building had not yet arrived at work when the truck bomb exploded, but 168 people were killed. Point out that the Oklahoma City bombing was the most deadly attack by domestic terrorists in U.S. history.

AS YOU READ Ask students to pay attention to the rhetorical devices used in this speech. How do they help the speaker advance his purpose?

 Common Core Support

- cite strong and thorough textual evidence
- analyze how an author's ideas are developed
- determine an author's point of view or purpose
- analyze how an author uses rhetoric to advance his or her purpose

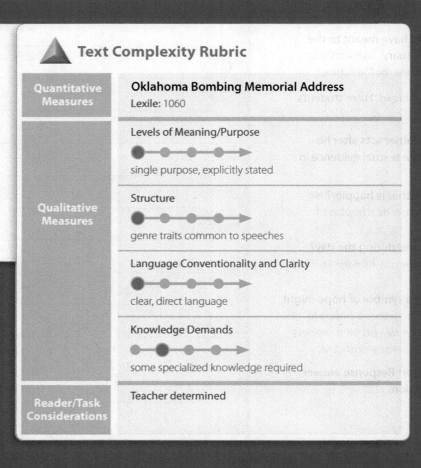

Text Complexity Rubric

Quantitative Measures

Oklahoma Bombing Memorial Address
Lexile: 1060

Qualitative Measures

Levels of Meaning/Purpose
single purpose, explicitly stated

Structure
genre traits common to speeches

Language Conventionality and Clarity
clear, direct language

Knowledge Demands
some specialized knowledge required

Reader/Task Considerations
Teacher determined

Analyze Author's Purpose and Rhetoric

Students should read this speech carefully all the way through. Close-reading questions at the bottom of the page will help them focus on a thorough analysis of the author's purpose. As they read, students should jot down comments or questions about the text in the margins.

WHEN STUDENTS STRUGGLE . . .

To help students analyze the "Oklahoma Bombing Memorial Address," have them work in small groups to fill out a chart like the one shown below.

CITE TEXT EVIDENCE For practice in analyzing an author's purpose and rhetoric, ask students to cite text evidence for each section of the chart.

Purpose	Rhetoric
to show support for the grieving	"Today our nation joins with you in grief." "We pledge to do all we can . . ." ". . . your pain is unimaginable, and we know that."
to thank those who helped	"We thank all those who have worked so heroically . . ." "Let us say clearly, they served us well, and we are grateful." ". . . many who left their own lives to come here . . ."
to connect with his audience	". . . also come as parents, as husband and wife . . ." ". . . we will stand with you for as many tomorrows as it takes." "My fellow Americans . . ."
to influence people's actions	". . . you must try to pay tribute to your loved ones . . ." "In the face of death, let us honor life." "The hurt you feel must not be allowed to turn into hate . . ."

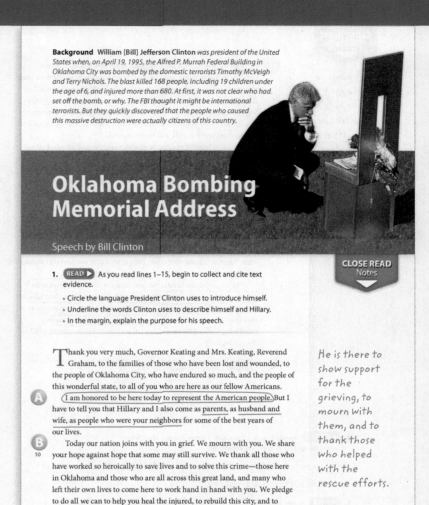

Background William [Bill] Jefferson Clinton *was president of the United States when, on April 19, 1995, the Alfred P. Murrah Federal Building in Oklahoma City was bombed by the domestic terrorists Timothy McVeigh and Terry Nichols. The blast killed 168 people, including 19 children under the age of 6, and injured more than 680. At first, it was not clear who had set off the bomb, or why. The FBI thought it might be international terrorists. But they quickly discovered that the people who caused this massive destruction were actually citizens of this country.*

Oklahoma Bombing Memorial Address

Speech by Bill Clinton

CLOSE READ Notes

1. **READ ▶** As you read lines 1–15, begin to collect and cite text evidence.

   • Circle the language President Clinton uses to introduce himself.
   • Underline the words Clinton uses to describe himself and Hillary.
   • In the margin, explain the purpose for his speech.

Thank you very much, Governor Keating and Mrs. Keating, Reverend Graham, to the families of those who have been lost and wounded, to the people of Oklahoma City, who have endured so much, and the people of this wonderful state, to all of you who are here as our fellow Americans.
(A) (I am honored to be here today to represent the American people.) But I have to tell you that Hillary and I also come as <u>parents</u>, as <u>husband and wife</u>, as <u>people who were your neighbors</u> for some of the best years of our lives.
(B) Today our nation joins with you in grief. We mourn with you. We share
10 your hope against hope that some may still survive. We thank all those who have worked so heroically to save lives and to solve this crime—those here in Oklahoma and those who are all across this great land, and many who left their own lives to come here to work hand in hand with you. We pledge to do all we can to help you heal the injured, to rebuild this city, and to bring to justice those who did this evil.

He is there to show support for the grieving, to mourn with them, and to thank those who helped with the rescue efforts.

19

1. **READ AND CITE TEXT EVIDENCE** Tell students that Clinton made his speech in Oklahoma City four days after the bombing took place. The people he names are the Governor of Oklahoma and his wife, and the Reverend Billy Graham, who also spoke at the memorial. Clinton had lived in—and been governor of—Arkansas, a state that adjoins Oklahoma.

(A) ASK STUDENTS to compare what they wrote describing the purpose of the speech. Have them cite the text evidence supporting their descriptions. *Students may point out that Clinton represents the American people (line 5), identifies with the people who suffered (lines 6–7), and thanks those who worked to help (lines 10–13). He promises to bring justice to those responsible (line 15).*

His purpose here is to acknowledge the tragedy and offer his sympathy.

C This terrible sin took the lives of our American family, innocent children in that building, only because their parents were trying to be good parents as well as good workers; citizens in the building going about their daily business; and many there who served the rest of us—who worked to help the elderly and the disabled, who worked to support our farmers and our veterans, who worked to enforce our laws and to protect us. Let us say clearly, they served us well, and we are grateful.

But for so many of you they were also neighbors and friends. You saw them at church or the PTA meetings, at the civic clubs, at the ball park. You know them in ways that all the rest of America could not. And to all the members of the families here present who have suffered loss, though we share your grief, your pain is unimaginable, and we know that. We cannot undo it. That is God's work.

Our words seem small beside the loss you have endured. But I found a few I wanted to share today. I've received a lot of letters in these last terrible days. **D** One stood out because it came from a young widow and a mother of three whose own husband was murdered with over 200 other Americans when Pan Am 103[1] was shot down. Here is what that woman said I should say to you today:

The anger you feel is valid, but you must not allow yourselves to be consumed by it. The hurt you feel must not be allowed to turn into hate, but instead into the search for justice. The loss you feel must not paralyze your own lives. Instead, you must try to pay tribute to your loved ones by continuing to do all the things they left undone, thus ensuring they did not die in vain.

[1] **Pan Am 103:** transatlantic flight from London to New York, bombed by terrorists over Lockerbie, Scotland, on December 21, 1988.

---

2. **◄ REREAD** Reread lines 9–15. Make an inference about why Clinton began his speech by speaking about grief.

Clinton wanted to connect emotionally with his audience, most of whom had suffered a great loss.

3. **READ ►** As you read lines 16–49, continue to cite textual evidence.

- Underline descriptive language that describes the tragedy.
- Circle examples of advice Clinton gave his audience.
- In the margin, explain Clinton's purpose in lines 16–28.

20

" You have lost too much, but you have not lost everything. "

Wise words from one who also knows.

You have lost too much, but you have not lost everything. And you have certainly not lost America, for we will stand with you for as many tomorrows as it takes.

If ever we needed evidence of that, I could only recall the words of Governor and Mrs. Keating: "If anybody thinks that Americans are mostly mean and selfish, they ought to come to Oklahoma. If anybody thinks Americans have lost the capacity for love and caring and courage, they ought to come to Oklahoma."

To all my fellow Americans beyond this hall, I say, one thing we owe those who have sacrificed is the duty to **purge** ourselves of the dark forces which gave rise to this evil. They are forces that threaten our common peace, our freedom, our way of life. Let us teach our children that the God of comfort is also the God of righteousness: Those who trouble their own house will inherit the wind. Justice will prevail.

E Let us let our own children know that we will stand against the forces of fear. When there is talk of hatred, let us stand up and talk against it. When there is talk of violence, let us stand up and talk against it. In the face of death, let us honor life. As St. Paul admonished us, Let us "not be overcome by evil, but overcome evil with good."

purge:
to purify; to rid of sin, guilt

admonished:
cautioned against

---

4. **◄ REREAD AND DISCUSS** Reread lines 29–40. With a small group, discuss why the letter from the widow stood out to Clinton and why he chose to include it in his speech.

5. **READ ►** As you read lines 50–74, underline the phrases that Clinton repeats.

21

---

2. **REREAD AND CITE TEXT EVIDENCE**

B ASK STUDENTS to infer what feelings most of Clinton's audience would have had just a few days after the bombing. *They would probably be shocked at what had happened in their city and devastated about the victims.* Why might Clinton have started his speech talking about their grief? *He wanted to first acknowledge their feelings and show that the nation supports them in their grief.*

3. **READ AND CITE TEXT EVIDENCE**

C ASK STUDENTS why Clinton identified the kinds of people who worked in the building and how they affected others' lives (lines 16–28). *Clinton describes the victims as parents, workers, and children. He then goes on to describe them in more personal terms, to show how they touched the lives of the people of Oklahoma.*

FOR ELL STUDENTS Explain to students that the abbreviation "PTA" in line 24 stands for Parent-Teacher Association.

4. **REREAD AND DISCUSS USING TEXT EVIDENCE**

D ASK STUDENTS why the letter from the widow had such an impact on Clinton. *The widow had overcome the extreme anger she would be expected to feel.* Why did Clinton include the widow's advice in his speech? *The advice came from someone who had been through a similar experience.*

5. **READ AND CITE TEXT EVIDENCE**

E ASK STUDENTS what effect the repetition has. *The repetition reinforces the idea that people are not alone.*

Critical Vocabulary: purge (line 51) Have students share their definitions of *purge*, and ask volunteers to use the verb.

Critical Vocabulary: admonished (line 59) Have students suggest several synonyms for the verb *admonish*. Possible synonyms are *warn, advise, encourage, recommend, exhort.*

Yesterday, Hillary and I had the privilege of speaking with some children of other federal employees—children like those who were lost here. And one little girl said something we will never forget. She said, "We should all plant a tree in memory of the children." So this morning before we got on the plane to come here, at the White House, we planted that tree in honor of the children of Oklahoma. It was a dogwood with its wonderful spring flower and its deep, enduring roots. It embodies the lesson of the Psalms[2]—that the life of a good person is like a tree whose leaf does not wither.

70   My fellow Americans, a tree takes a long time to grow, and wounds take a long time to heal. But we must begin. Those who are lost now belong to God. Some day we will be with them. But until that happens, their legacy must be our lives.

Thank you all, and God bless you.

[2] **Psalms:** a section of the Bible.

6. ◀ REREAD AND DISCUSS Reread lines 61–74. With a small group, discuss Clinton's story of the tree. What does the tree symbolize? Why does he mention the planting of the tree to his audience?

SHORT RESPONSE

Cite Text Evidence Do you think Clinton's speech was effective in showing support for the American people during this tragedy? How does his use of language and parallelism help advance his purpose? Explain, **citing text evidence** in your response.

Possible response: Clinton's speech was very effective. He shared the grief of those who had lost loved ones, those affected by the tragedy, and all of the United States citizens. At the same time, he appealed to the people to follow the values they have as Americans, and he read a message from a woman whose husband had been killed in a terrorist bombing, exhorting people not to be "consumed" by anger, but to "search for justice." By demonstrating a deep understanding of people's feelings and giving advice for moving on, he made an emotional connection to all who heard him.

22

---

6. REREAD AND CITE TEXT EVIDENCE

F **ASK STUDENTS** to look closely at what the girl suggested, what the Clintons did, and what a tree symbolizes. Have groups share their responses. *Students may point out that the Clintons planted a tree in memory at the White House, to honor the children in the nation's symbolic center. Clinton points out that "a tree takes a long time to grow" and compares that time with wounds that take a long time to heal. He says that we have to begin healing, and planting the tree is a symbolic beginning.*

SHORT RESPONSE

Cite Text Evidence Students' responses should include text evidence that supports their positions. They should:

- determine whether or not they find the speech effective.
- give examples of rhetorical devices that further Clinton's points.
- explain Clinton's use of parallelism to evoke emotions.

TO CHALLENGE STUDENTS . . .

When Clinton made the "Oklahoma Bombing Memorial Address," the audience did not know who was responsible for the terrorist act. Many people assumed that it was international terrorists.

ASK STUDENTS to reread the speech and discuss whether or not any passages might have been worded differently had it been common knowledge that the crime was committed by an American. *Students may suggest that the passages that include "our American family" (line 16) and "If anybody thinks that Americans are mostly mean" (lines 46–47) might have been worded differently. They might suggest that Clinton would have included specific thoughts and advice about dealing with domestic terrorism.*

DIG DEEPER

With the class, return to Question 4, Reread and Discuss. Have groups share their responses to the question.

ASK STUDENTS about the letter that Clinton shared with his audience.

- Have students discuss why the widow's words were relevant in the situation. *She had lost her husband in a terrorist attack and must have felt the same emotions that people in Oklahoma City were feeling.*
- Ask students why Clinton thought that the widow's advice was meaningful. *People's anger could turn to hate, but that would not solve anything. The widow pointed out that hate could ruin the lives of the survivors.*
- Ask students what effect the widow's letter might have had on the audience. *The letter from the widow showed that someone who had gone through a similar experience had coped and been able to live through the pain. The letter might have given the survivors hope.*

ASK STUDENTS to return to their Short Response answer and revise it based on the class discussion.

The Struggle for Freedom

The Struggle for Freedom

"If there is no struggle, there is no progress."

—Frederick Douglass

SPEECH

A Eulogy for
Dr. Martin Luther King Jr.   **Robert F. Kennedy**

SHORT STORY

The Prisoner Who Wore Glasses   **Bessie Head**

A Eulogy for Dr. Martin Luther King Jr.

For additional background, students can view the video "Class of the 20th Century: 1963–1968" in their eBooks.

Speech by Robert F. Kennedy

Why This Text

Speeches are meant to be heard, not read; sometimes, however, the message is so timely and the messenger so powerful that the meaning comes through even in print. Readers of Kennedy's eulogy, moved as they are by its passion, will nonetheless appreciate its brilliance as a speech, well worthy of the great orator being eulogized. With the help of the close-reading questions, students will examine this speech in terms of its craft and context in order to better understand its place in our shared history.

Background Have students read the background and information about Robert Kennedy, including the circumstances surrounding the eulogy. Kennedy, knowing how unprepared people would be to hear this terrible news, chose his words carefully, as they had to accomplish several things at once— convey a sense of shared grief, pay homage to the great Dr. King, and, importantly, give hope to a people still reeling from the shock of his own brother's murder.

AS YOU READ Ask students to pay attention to the rhetorical devices used to advance the purpose of the speech. How do they help the speaker connect to his audience?

 ## Common Core Support

- cite strong and thorough textual evidence
- analyze how an author's ideas are developed
- determine an author's point of view
- analyze how an author uses rhetoric to advance his or her purpose

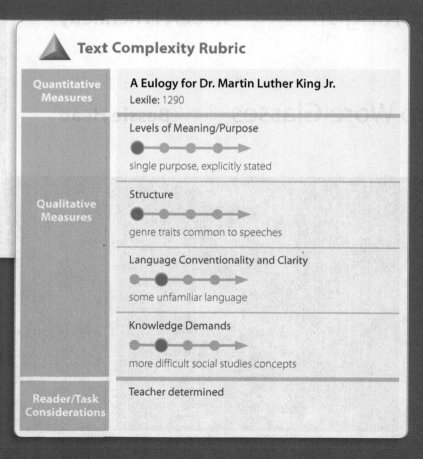

Text Complexity Rubric

Quantitative Measures

A Eulogy for Dr. Martin Luther King Jr.
Lexile: 1290

Qualitative Measures

Levels of Meaning/Purpose
single purpose, explicitly stated

Structure
genre traits common to speeches

Language Conventionality and Clarity
some unfamiliar language

Knowledge Demands
more difficult social studies concepts

Reader/Task Considerations
Teacher determined

Strategies for CLOSE READING

Analyze Rhetorical Devices

Students should read this speech carefully all the way through. Close-reading questions at the bottom of the page will help them focus on a thorough analysis of the rhetorical devices the author uses to advance his point of view. As they read, students should jot down comments or questions about the text in the margins.

WHEN STUDENTS STRUGGLE . . .

To help students analyze the text of Kennedy's eulogy for Dr. King, have them work in small groups to fill out a chart like the one shown below.

CITE TEXT EVIDENCE For practice in identifying examples of rhetorical devices, ask students to cite text evidence for each feature.

Device	Example
Repetition	"In this difficult day, in this difficult time . . ." "What we need in the United States is not division; what we need in the United States is not hatred . . ."
Parallelism	". . . what kind of nation . . ." ". . . white people amongst white . . ." "We will have difficult times . . . it is not the end of disorder."

Background On April 4, 1968, hundreds of African Americans gathered in Indianapolis, Indiana, for what they thought would be an exciting political event. Presidential candidate **Robert F. Kennedy** was coming to speak to them. Before he was to deliver his speech, Kennedy was informed that civil rights leader Martin Luther King Jr. had been assassinated earlier that day. Kennedy nevertheless went to the rally, where he found the audience upbeat in anticipation of his appearance. Realizing they were unaware of the tragic events, he began his speech with the following words.

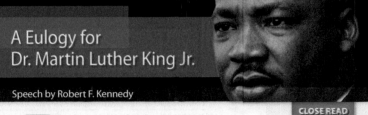

A Eulogy for Dr. Martin Luther King Jr.

Speech by Robert F. Kennedy

CLOSE READ
Notes

1. **READ ▶** As you read lines 1–13, begin to collect and cite text evidence.

- Underline examples of repetition and parallelism.
- In the margin, note what questions Kennedy poses.

I have bad news <u>for</u> you, <u>for</u> all of our fellow citizens, and people who love peace all over the world, and that is that Martin Luther King was shot and killed tonight.

Martin Luther King dedicated his life to love and to justice for his fellow human beings, and he died because of that effort.

B <u>In this difficult</u> day, <u>in this difficult</u> time for the United States, it is perhaps well to ask <u>what</u> kind of a nation we are and <u>what</u> direction we want to move in. For those of you who are black—considering the evidence there evidently is that there were white people who were responsible—
10 you can be filled <u>with bitterness, with hatred</u>, and a desire for revenge. We can move in that direction as a country, in great polarization—<u>black people amongst black, white people amongst white</u>, filled with hatred
A toward one another.

He asks what kind of nation are we and in what direction do we want to move.

25

1. **READ AND CITE TEXT EVIDENCE** Tell students that repetition works to reinforce the speaker's message and create a strong link in the mind of the listener. Here, it may have had another purpose—to create a mood.

A **ASK STUDENTS** to describe the effect this repetition might have had on a roomful of hurt and angry people. Have students cite an example from the text. *Students may cite "In this difficult day, in this difficult time..." (line 6) as an example of the gentle, soothing effect repetition can have on an audience in shock, like a parent comforting a scared child.*

CLOSE READ
Notes

Martin Luther King Jr., leader of the Southern Christian Leadership Council; Attorney General Robert Kennedy; Roy Wilkins, Executive Secretary of the NAACP; and Vice President Lyndon Johnson after a special White House conference on civil rights (June 1963).

C Or we can make an effort, as Martin Luther King did, to understand and to comprehend, and to replace that violence, that stain of bloodshed that has spread across our land, with an effort to understand with compassion and love.

For those of you who are black and are tempted to be filled with hatred and distrust at the injustice of such an act, against all white people, I can
20 only say that I feel in my own heart the same kind of feeling. I had a member of my family killed, but he was killed by a white man. But we have to make an effort in the United States, we have to make an effort to understand, to go beyond these rather difficult times.

My favorite poet was Aeschylus. He wrote, "In our sleep, pain which cannot forget falls drop by drop upon the heart until, in our own despair, against our will, comes wisdom through the awful grace of God."

2. **◄ REREAD** Reread lines 6–13. How does Kennedy use parallelism to emphasize the potential for American society to become more divided?

Kennedy's use of parallelism emphasizes the unity of the American
society in "what kind of nation we are and what direction we want
to move" and contrasts that with division in "black people amongst
black, white people amongst white."

3. **READ ►** As you read lines 14–26, underline the options Kennedy offers his audience.

26

CLOSE READ
Notes

> *We will have difficult times. We've had difficult times in the past. We will have difficult times in the future.*

E What we need in the United States is not division; what we need in the United States is not hatred; what we need in the United States is not violence or lawlessness but love and wisdom, and compassion toward one another,
30 and a feeling of justice towards those who still suffer within our country, whether they be white or they be black.

So I shall ask you tonight to return home, to say a prayer for the family of Martin Luther King, that's true, but more importantly to say a prayer for our own country, which all of us love—a prayer for understanding and that compassion of which I spoke.

We can do well in this country. We will have difficult times. We've had difficult times in the past. We will have difficult times in the future. It is not the end of violence; it is not the end of lawlessness; it is not the end of disorder.

4. **◄ REREAD** Reread lines 18–23. What is Kennedy referring to when he says he "had a member of my family killed . . ."?

Robert Kennedy's brother John F. Kennedy was assassinated in Dallas
while he was President of the United States.

5. **READ ►** As you read lines 27–46, underline the advice that Kennedy gives to his audience.

27

---

2. **REREAD AND CITE TEXT EVIDENCE**

B **ASK STUDENTS** why, in lines 6–13, Kennedy suggested that it was possible that black people would be full of bitterness and hatred and a desire for revenge. *He personally understood the instinct to feel hatred and bitterness, but wanted to show why it would lead to a divided nation.*

3. **READ AND CITE TEXT EVIDENCE**

C **ASK STUDENTS** why Kennedy might have brought in Martin Luther King's ideas at this point in the speech. *He wanted to remind people that King was a man of peace; he wanted them to carry on his legacy and replace violence with compassion.*

FOR ELL STUDENTS The verb *comprehend* is very close to its false Spanish cognate *comprender* (to understand). Point out that *comprehend* goes beyond understanding—it means grasping the importance, nature, or significance of something.

4. **REREAD AND CITE TEXT EVIDENCE**

D **ASK STUDENTS** why Kennedy made reference to the murder of his brother in lines 20–21. *He wanted people to know he had experienced a similar, shocking loss; he was speaking from the heart, as a human being rather than a public figure.*

5. **READ AND CITE TEXT EVIDENCE**

E **ASK STUDENTS** to summarize the advice that Kennedy gives in lines 27–46. *He advises people to act with love rather than hate, and to pray not only for the King family, but for understanding and compassion.*

FOR ELL STUDENTS Encourage students to analyze the double suffix in the word *lawlessness*. Have them work from the base word *law*, and ask volunteers what meaning each of the suffixes (-less, -ness) adds to the word.

F 40   But the vast majority of white people and the vast majority of black
people in this country want to live together, want to improve the quality of
our life, and want justice for all human beings who abide in our land.
        Let us dedicate ourselves to what the Greeks wrote so many years ago:
to tame the savageness of man and to make gentle the life of this world.
        Let us dedicate ourselves to that, and say a prayer for our country and
for our people.

6. ◀ REREAD AND DISCUSS With a small group, discuss the central idea
    Kennedy brings up in his speech. Do you think it's an effective eulogy?
    Do you think it adequately honored Dr. King?

SHORT RESPONSE

Cite Text Evidence How does Kennedy's use of rhetoric advance his
argument? How does his use of parallelism help speak to a racially divided
audience? **Cite evidence** from the text in your reponse.

Kennedy uses repetition—especially of the word "difficult"—to
make his argument inclusive; he lets his audience know that he is
aware of the problems they all face. The fact that his own brother
was also assassinated strengthens his argument, as he can identify
with the feelings of those who are angry about Martin Luther King's
murder. Kennedy strengthens his argument by appealing to people's
better natures, and points out that all people want the same things:
quality of life and justice for all human beings.

28

6. REREAD AND DISCUSS USING TEXT EVIDENCE

F ASK STUDENTS to look closely at the themes Kennedy
keeps coming back to in his eulogy. Have groups share their
responses. *Students may point out that Kennedy effectively defused
a potentially inflammatory situation by repeatedly returning to the
ideals King stood for and the importance of continuing his work as a
way of honoring him.*

SHORT RESPONSE

Cite Text Evidence Students should:

- determine whether or not they find the eulogy effective.
- give examples of rhetorical devices that further Kennedy's
  purpose.
- cite text evidence in their response.

TO CHALLENGE STUDENTS . . .

To deepen students' understanding, ask students to search for a
video of the eulogy online.

ASK STUDENTS how hearing the eulogy added dimension to
the printed word. How important was it to hear the audience
reaction? How well did Kennedy handle the situation? Did the
speech match, or exceed, their expectations? *The audience
reaction gives you a sense of the awesome responsibility Kennedy
had. Although visibly shaken himself, he succeeded in offering
comfort to a stunned audience. Lines such as "I had a member of my
family killed. . . by a white man," although emotionally shocking, were
intended to reinforce a sense of unity*

DIG DEEPER

With the class, return to Question 6, Reread and Discuss. Have
groups share their responses to the question.

ASK STUDENTS about the way Kennedy handled a very tough
situation.

- Have students think about Kennedy's audience. Why had
  they come to the event? What did they expect to hear? Why
  do you think Kennedy began his speech the way he did? *The
  people were supporters of Kennedy's run for the presidency—no
  one expected this horrible news. Kennedy started his speech in a
  very blunt, no-nonsense manner. He did not euphemize: he used
  words like "shot" and killed," possibly with the idea that directness
  is the most respectful way to present this kind of information.*

- Ask students how the tone of the speech was meant to
  help people deal with this crisis. *The rhythm and cadence
  of Kennedy's speech was meant to have a soothing effect and
  impart a feeling of solemnity.*

- Ask students how Kennedy used King's ideas to help bring
  people together. *Kennedy knew that people might simply search
  for revenge; some might blame all white people for the acts of
  one. Kennedy tried to convey the idea that this was not what King
  would have wanted; he tried to persuade people that the best
  way to honor King was to follow the principles he espoused, and
  for which he died: "to make gentle the life of this world."*

ASK STUDENTS to return to their Short Response answer and
revise it based on the class discussion.

The Prisoner Who Wore Glasses

Short Story by Bessie Head

Why This Text

Students sometimes read a story without analyzing the cultural background of the author. "The Prisoner Who Wore Glasses" is set in South Africa during apartheid. The story's message is better understood and appreciated when analyzed in the context of the author's historical and cultural background. With the help of the close-reading questions, students will interpret the central message of Head's story. This close reading will lead students to effectively read world literature.

Background Have students read the background and the information about the author. "The Prisoner Who Wore Glasses" is a story set in South Africa that revolves around themes of discrimination, resilience of the human spirit, and the ability of people to bridge racial gaps through cooperation. Introduce the selection by telling students that as the daughter of a white woman and a black man, Head experienced racism in South Africa firsthand.

AS YOU READ Ask students to analyze the cultural experience presented in this story from outside the United States. Which details are clues that the story is not set in the United States?

Common Core Support

- cite strong and thorough textual evidence
- analyze how complex characters develop over the course of a text
- analyze an author's choices concerning how to structure a text
- analyze a point of view or cultural experience from outside the United States

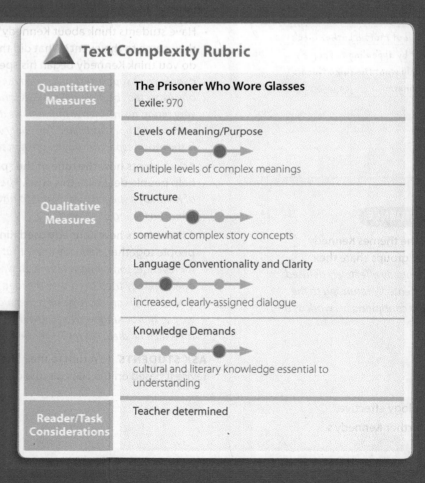

Text Complexity Rubric

Quantitative Measures

The Prisoner Who Wore Glasses
Lexile: 970

Qualitative Measures

Levels of Meaning/Purpose

multiple levels of complex meanings

Structure

somewhat complex story concepts

Language Conventionality and Clarity

increased, clearly-assigned dialogue

Knowledge Demands

cultural and literary knowledge essential to understanding

Reader/Task Considerations

Teacher determined

Analyze Point of View: Cultural Background

Students should read this story carefully all the way through. Close-reading questions at the bottom of the page will help them focus on a thorough analysis of the story. As they read, students should jot down comments or questions about the text in the side margins.

WHEN STUDENTS STRUGGLE . . .

To help students analyze the author's cultural background, have them work in a small group to fill out a chart, such as the one shown below, as they analyze the text.

CITE TEXT EVIDENCE For practice in analyzing a cultural point of view, ask students to cite details from the text that reflect specific cultural context that adds to the plot.

Detail	How It Adds to the Plot
The men in Span One are political prisoners.	They have not committed crimes.
Black warders cannot be in charge of Span One.	The political prisoners must be in favor of black equality.
Brille stands up to the white warder Hannetjie.	Brille is making a symbolic stand against apartheid.
The black prisoners work together with the white warder in cooperation.	The system of apartheid could be overcome by cooperation between the sides.

Background *Apartheid—systematic racial segregation—was initiated in South Africa in 1948 when* **Bessie Head** *was eleven years old. Under apartheid's rigid classification system, she was designated a "colored" person and was denied the full privileges of citizenship in her homeland. Raised from birth by a child welfare agency, she was later placed with foster parents. After training in a missionary school, she worked as a teacher and journalist before emigrating to Botswana, a neighboring country that was then under British rule. Many of her writings explore the tragedies and injustices of South Africa under apartheid rule.*

The Prisoner Who Wore Glasses

Short Story by Bessie Head

CLOSE READ
Notes

1. **READD** As you read lines 1–24, begin to collect and cite text evidence.

- Underline language that describes the prisoner.
- Circle text that describes the warder.
- In the margin, summarize the descriptions.

Scarcely a breath of wind disturbed the stillness of the day and the long rows of cabbages were bright green in the sunlight. Large white clouds drifted slowly across the deep blue sky. Now and then they obscured the sun and caused a chill on the backs of the prisoners who had to work all day long in the cabbage field. This trick the clouds were playing with the sun eventually caused one of the prisoners who wore glasses to stop work, straighten up and peer short-sightedly at them. He was a thin little fellow with a hollowed-out chest and comic knobbly knees. He also had a lot of fanciful ideas because he smiled at the clouds.

10   "Perhaps they want me to send a message to the children," he thought, tenderly, noting that the clouds were drifting in the direction of his home some hundred miles away. But before he could frame the message, the warder in charge of his work span[1] shouted: "Hey, what do you think you're doing, Brille?"

[1] **work span:** a group or unit of workers.

The prisoner is physically unthreatening. He also has a good imagination.

29

1. **READ AND CITE TEXT EVIDENCE** Invite students to begin to analyze the characters of the prisoner and the warder.

A **ASK STUDENTS** to cite evidence to support their summaries of the text that describes the prisoner and the warder. *Students should cite evidence from lines 6–11 and lines 15–16 to support their descriptions of the prisoner, and lines 13–14 and 17–18 to support their descriptions of the warder.*

The warder is cold, brutal, and inhuman.

The prisoner swung round, blinking rapidly, yet at the same time sizing up the enemy. He was a new warder, named Jacobus Stephanus Hannetjie. His eyes were the color of the sky but they were frightening. A simple, primitive, brutal soul gazed out of them. The prisoner bent down quickly and a message was quietly passed down the line: "We're in for trouble this

20 time, comrades."

"Why?" rippled back up the line.

"Because he's not human" the reply rippled down and yet only the crunching of the spades as they turned over the earth disturbed the stillness.

This particular work span was known as Span One. It was composed of ten men and they were all political prisoners. They were grouped together for convenience as it was one of the prison regulations that no black warder should be in charge of a political prisoner lest this prisoner convert him to his view. It never seemed to occur to the authorities that this very reasoning

30 was the strength of Span One and a clue to the strange terror they aroused in the warders. As political prisoners they were unlike the other prisoners in the sense that they felt no guilt nor were they outcasts of society. All guilty men instinctively cower, which was why it was the kind of prison where men got knocked out cold with a blow at the back of the head from an iron bar. Up until the arrival of Warder Hannetjie, no warder had dared beat any member of Span One and no warder had lasted more than a

2. ◀ REREAD ▶ Reread lines 12–20. State the conflict in your own words.

The prisoner's work span has been taken over by a brutal white
warder.

3. READ ▶ As you read lines 25–42, continue to cite textual evidence.

• Underline descriptions of Span One.
• Circle adjectives that describe why Span One is unique.

week with them. The battle was entirely psychological. Span One was assertive and it was beyond the scope of white warders to handle assertive black men. Thus, Span One had got out of control. They were the best

40 thieves and liars in the camp. They lived all day on raw cabbages. They chatted and smoked tobacco. And since they moved, thought, and acted as one, they had perfected every technique of group concealment.

Trouble began that very day between Span One and Warder Hannetjie. It was because of the short-sightedness of Brille. That was the nickname he was given in prison and is the Afrikaans[2] word for someone who wears glasses. Brille could never judge the approach of the prison gates and on several occasions he had munched on cabbages and dropped them almost at the feet of the warder and all previous warders had overlooked this. Not so Warder Hannetjie.

50 "Who dropped that cabbage?" he thundered.

Brille stepped out of line.

"I did," he said meekly.

"All right," said Hannetjie. "The whole Span goes three meals off."

"But I told you I did it," Brille protested.

The blood rushed to Warder Hannetjie's face.

"Look 'ere," he said. "I don't take orders from a kaffir.[3] I don't know

[2] **Afrikaans:** a South African language that developed from Dutch.
[3] **kaffir:** a disparaging term for a black African.

4. ◀ REREAD ▶ Reread lines 25–42. How does the author foreshadow trouble in the prison? Support your answer with explicit textual evidence.

The author describes the special treatment given to the prisoners in
Span One and explains that "no warder had lasted more than a week
with them."

5. READ ▶ As you read lines 43–102, continue to cite textual evidence.

• Underline the text that hints at racial conflict.
• Circle words that show a shift from the present to the past.
• In the margin of lines 73–94, explain what Brille remembers.

---

2. **REREAD AND CITE TEXT EVIDENCE**

Ⓑ **ASK STUDENTS** to cite evidence that supports their statement of the story's conflict. *Students should cite text that describes Hannetjie (lines 12–14 and lines 17–18) and text that explains Brille's assessment of Hannetjie (lines 19–20).*

3. **READ AND CITE TEXT EVIDENCE**

Ⓒ **ASK STUDENTS** to cite text evidence showing that Span One is unique. *Students should cite that Span One was a group of "political" prisoners (line 28). They should cite adjectives such as strange (line 30) and unlike (line 31). The adjective assertive describes how they are unique (line 38). The superlative adjective best (line 39) is another clue that Span One is unique.*

FOR ELL STUDENTS Review that the verb *swung* is the past and past participle of the irregular verb *to swing*, which means "to move vigorously through a wide arc or circle."

4. **REREAD AND CITE TEXT EVIDENCE**

Ⓓ **ASK STUDENTS** to cite text evidence to support their explanation of how the author foreshadows that there will be trouble in the prison. *Students should cite evidence of Span One getting special treatment (lines 35–36 and lines 40–42) and evidence that they frequently have conflict with warders (lines 36–37).*

5. **READ AND CITE TEXT EVIDENCE**

Ⓔ **ASK STUDENTS** to cite textual evidence to support their explanation of what Brille remembers. *Students should cite text that describes the violence that occurred in his own home, such as lines 83–85. They should cite evidence that describes the effect this violence had on his life, such as lines 90–91.*

FOR ELL STUDENTS Explain that the expression "blood rushed to (someone's) face" means that the person is embarrassed and her face turns red.

what kind of kaffir you think you are. Why don't you say Baas. I'm your Baas, Why don't you say Baas, hey?"

Brille blinked his eyes rapidly but by contrast his voice was strangely
60 calm.

(F) "I'm twenty years older than you," he said. It was the first thing that came to mind but the comrades seemed to think it a huge joke. A titter swept up the line. The next thing Warder Hannetjie whipped out a knobkerrie and gave Brille several blows about the head. What surprised his comrades was the speed with which Brille had removed his glasses or else they would have been smashed to pieces on the ground. That evening in the cell Brille was very apologetic.

"I'm sorry, comrades," he said. "I've put you into a hell of a mess."

"Never mind, brother," they said. "What happens to one of us, happens
70 to all."

"I'll try to make up for it, comrades," he said. "I'll steal something so that you don't go hungry."

(J) Privately, Brille was very philosophical about his head wounds. It was the first time an act of violence had been perpetrated against him but he had long been a witness of extreme, almost unbelievable human brutality. He had twelve children and his mind traveled back that evening through the sixteen years of **bedlam** in which he had lived. It had all happened in a small, drab little three-bedroomed house in a small, drab little street in the Eastern Cape, and the children kept coming year after year because neither
80 he nor Martha ever managed the contraceptives the right way, and a teacher's salary never allowed moving to a bigger house, and he was always taking exams to improve his salary only to have it all eaten up by hungry
(E) mouths. Everything was pretty horrible, especially the way the children fought. They'd get hold of each other's heads and give them a good bashing against the wall. Martha gave up somewhere along the line so they worked out a thing between them. The bashings, biting and blood were to operate in full swing until he came home. He was to be the bogeyman and when it worked he never failed to have a sense of godhead at the way in which his presence could change savages into fairly reasonable human beings.
90 Yet somehow it was this chaos and mismanagement at the center of his life that drove him into politics. It was really an ordered, beautiful world with just a few basic slogans to learn along with the rights of mankind. At one stage, before things became very bad, there were conferences to attend, all very far away from home.

bedlam:
chaos;
complete
disorder

Brille
remembers
the violence
that occurred
in his own
home. His
chaotic
homelife led
him toward
politics.

32

"Let's face it," he thought ruefully. "I'm only learning right now what it means to be a politician. All this while I've been running away from Martha and the kids."

And the pain in his head brought a hard lump to his throat. That was what the children did to each other daily and Martha wasn't managing and
100 if Warder Hannetjie had not interrupted him that morning he would have sent the following message: "Be good comrades, my children. Cooperate, then life will run smoothly."

(G) The next day Warder Hannetjie, caught this old man of twelve children stealing grapes from the farm shed. They were an enormous quantity of grapes in a ten-gallon tin and for this misdeed the old man spent a week in the isolation cell. In fact, Span One as a whole was in constant trouble. Warder Hannetjie seemed to have eyes at the back of his head. He uncovered the trick about the cabbages, how they were split in two with the spade and immediately covered with earth and then unearthed again and
110 eaten with split-second timing. He found out how tobacco smoke was beaten into the ground and he found out how conversations were whispered down the wind.

For about two weeks Span One lived in acute misery. The cabbages, tobacco, and conversations had been the **pivot** of jail life to them. Then one evening they noticed that their good old comrade who wore the glasses was looking rather pleased with himself. He pulled out a four-ounce packet of

pivot:
central point
on which
something else
depends

6. ◀ REREAD   Reread the dialogue between Brille and Hannetjie (lines 50–62). From what you know about apartheid, make an inference about why Brille stands up to Hannetjie.

When Brille stands up to the warder, his action is symbolic; it's as if black South Africans are standing up to the white minority and taking back their dignity.

7. READ ▶   As you read lines 103–138, continue to cite textual evidence.
   • Underline the crimes Hannetjie uncovers.
   • Circle the text that describes a turning point of the story.
   • Underline text that refers to Brille as a father.

33

Critical Vocabulary: bedlam (line 77) Ask students to share their definitions of *bedlam*. Ask them to explain how Head's choice of the word *bedlam* impacts meaning in this paragraph. *Answers will vary. Students might say that by choosing a word associated with insanity, Head is commenting on the result of exposure to constant violence.*

FOR ELL STUDENTS Review the meaning of the prefix *mis-*. Point out the word *mismanagement* in line 90. Then ask a volunteer to supply the base word, its meaning, and what meaning the prefix adds to it. *The word* mismanagement *means "supervision of a project done badly or wrongly."*

6. REREAD AND CITE TEXT EVIDENCE

   (F) **ASK STUDENTS** to read aloud and discuss their response with a partner. After their discussions, allow students to rewrite their response and add specific textual evidence.

7. READ AND CITE TEXT EVIDENCE   Point out to students that the development of Hannetjie and Brille's relationship moves the plot forward.

   (G) **ASK STUDENTS** to cite evidence that shows that Hannetjie and Brille have something in common. *Students should point out that they have both been punished for stealing (lines 103–104 and lines 124–126 and 138).*

   Critical Vocabulary: pivot (line 114) Ask students to compare definitions of *pivot*. Ask them to determine the meaning of *pivot* as it is used in the story.

tobacco by way of explanation and the comrades fell upon it with great greed. Brille merely smiled. After all, he was the father of many children. But when the last shred had disappeared, it occurred to the comrades that

120 they ought to be puzzled. Someone said: "I say, brother. We're watched like hawks these days. Where did you get the tobacco?"

"Hannetjie gave it to me," said Brille.

There was a long silence. Into it dropped a quiet bombshell.

"I saw Hannetjie in the shed today," and the failing eyesight blinked rapidly. "I caught him in the act of stealing five bags of fertilizer and he bribed me to keep my mouth shut."

There was another long silence.

"Prison is an evil life," Brille continued, apparently discussing some irrelevant matter. "It makes a man contemplate all kinds of evil deeds."

130 He held out his hand and closed it.

"You know, comrades," he said. "I've got Hannetjie. I'll betray him tomorrow."

Everyone began talking at once.

"Forget it, brother. You'll get shot."

Brille laughed.

"I won't," he said. "That is what I mean about evil. I am a father of children and I saw today that Hannetjie is just a child and stupidly truthful. I'm going to punish him severely because we need a good warder."

The following day, with Brille as witness, Hannetjie confessed to the

140 theft of the fertilizer and was fined a large sum of money. From then on Span One did very much as they pleased while Warder Hannetjie stood by and said nothing. But it was Brille who carried this to extremes. One day, at

8. **REREAD** Reread lines 113–138. Why does the author keep mentioning Brille's role as a father? Support your answer with explicit textual evidence.

The author is making the point that the prisoners and the warden all act like children. As Brille plans to punish Hannetjie he says, "I am a father of children and I saw today that Hannetjie is just a child.."

9. **READ** As you read lines 139–183, underline text that describes how life changes for Brille, Hannetjie, and Span One. In the margin, explain how Brille betrays Hannetjie.

34

> **Brille looked at him, for the first time struck with pity, and guilt.**

the close of work Warder Hannetjie said: "Brille, pick up my jacket and carry it back to the camp."

"But nothing in the regulations says I'm your servant, Hannetjie," Brille replied coolly.

"I've told you not to call me Hannetjie. You must say Baas," but Warder Hannetjie's voice lacked conviction. In turn, Brille squinted up at him.

"I'll tell you something about this Baas business, Hannetjie," he said.

150 "One of these days we are going to run the country. You are going to clean my car. Now, I have a fifteen-year-old son and I'd die of shame if you had to tell him that I ever called you Baas."

Warder Hannetjie went red in the face and picked up his coat.

On another occasion Brille was seen to be walking about the prison yard, openly smoking tobacco. On being taken before the prison commander he claimed to have received the tobacco from Warder Hannetjie. Throughout the tirade from his chief, Warder Hannetjie failed to defend himself but his nerve broke completely. He called Brille to one side.

"Brille," he said. "This thing between you and me must end. You may

160 not know it but I have a wife and children and you're driving me to suicide."

"Why don't you like your own medicine, Hannetjie?" Brille asked quietly.

"I can give you anything you want," Warder Hannetjie said in desperation.

"It's not only me but the whole of Span One," said Brille, cunningly. "The whole of Span One wants something from you."

Warder Hannetjie brightened with relief.

"I think I can manage if it's tobacco you want," he said.

Brille looked at him, for the first time struck with pity, and guilt.

Brille witnesses the warder's theft and gets him in trouble. Brille stands up to Hannetjie and even makes up stories that get him in trouble with his superiors.

35

---

8. **REREAD AND CITE TEXT EVIDENCE**

H **ASK STUDENTS** to trade their written response with a partner for a peer review. Partners should work together to improve their responses, and then rewrite their answers with specific textual evidence. *Students may cite evidence from line 118 or lines 136–138 to show that Brille has realized that the prisoners and the warder all act like children.*

9. **READ AND CITE TEXT EVIDENCE**

I **ASK STUDENTS** to cite text evidence to support their description of how life changes for Brille, Hannetjie, and Span One, as well as their explanation of how Brille betrays Hannetjie. *Students should cite evidence from lines 139–142 to show that Span One "did very much as they pleased" after the trial, and lines 149–152 that show how the relationship between the two men changed. Lines 179–181 show that Span One responded to the changes around them by "being the best work span in the camp."*

WHEN STUDENTS STRUGGLE . . .

To help students analyze the developments in the relationship between Brille and Hannetjie, have small groups work together to read aloud lines 139–183 as a script. Assign parts to a narrator, Warder Hannetjie, and Brille.

CITE TEXT EVIDENCE After reading the text aloud, have small groups cite specific lines that show a change in their relationship, such as lines 139–142 (showing that Hannetjie now says nothing when Span One acts out) or lines 147–148 (showing that Hannetjie's voice has lost its conviction). Ask them to explain what the evidence shows.

FOR ELL STUDENTS Point out that the word *tirade* should not be confused with *tired*, though they may sound similar to them. Explain that *tirade* is a long and angry speech.

CLOSE READ
Notes

170 He wondered if he had carried the whole business too far. The man was really a child.

"It's not tobacco we want, but you," he said. "We want you on our side. We want a good warder because without a good warder we won't be able to manage the long stretch ahead."

Warder Hannetjie interpreted this request in his own fashion and <u>his interpretation of what was good and human often left the prisoners of Span One speechless with surprise. He had a way of slipping off his revolver and picking up a spade and digging alongside Span One. He had a way of producing unheard of luxuries like boiled eggs from his farm nearby and</u>

180 things like cigarettes, and Span One responded nobly and got the reputation of being the best work span in the camp. And it wasn't only take from their side. They were awfully good at stealing certain commodities like fertilizer which were needed on the farm of Warder Hannetjie.

10. ◀ **REREAD AND DISCUSS** Reread lines 170–183. With a small group, analyze the parallels between Brille's relationships with his twelve children and his relationships with Hannetjie and Span One. Why did the author choose to include Brille's flashback about life with his wife and children?

SHORT RESPONSE

Cite Text Evidence Head's writing has been described as "having the dimensions of a parable"—a short, simple story illustrating a moral or spiritual truth. What simple truth does Head illustrate in "The Prisoner Who Wore Glasses"? Why is it particularly meaningful given her cultural point of view? **Cite text evidence** from the story.

> "Cooperate, then life will run smoothly," is the simple truth transmitted in "The Prisoner Who Wore Glasses." Head illustrates this truth by putting black political prisoners and a brutal white warder at odds. It takes a philosophical father figure with "a lot of fanciful ideas" to bring about cooperation. He sees warder and inmates alike as he sees his children: in need of management and firm discipline. Although the injustice of apartheid is the backdrop of the story, Head's message about cooperation and respect is accessible to everyone.

36

---

10. **REREAD AND DISCUSS USING TEXT EVIDENCE** Refer students to the flashback on page 32, lines 73–102.

J ASK STUDENTS to be ready to cite textual evidence to support their analysis of the parallels between Brille's relationships with his twelve children and his relationships with Hannetjie and Span One. *Students should recognize parallels in the violence between his children and Brille's role as disciplinarian.*

SHORT RESPONSE

Cite Text Evidence Student responses will vary, but they should cite evidence from the story to support their responses. Students should:

- state the moral of the story.
- cite text evidence that supports their response.
- analyze Head's cultural point of view.

TO CHALLENGE STUDENTS . . .

For more context, students can research apartheid in South Africa from 1948 through 1991.

ASK STUDENTS to relate how their research helped them analyze Head's cultural experience as it is reflected in "The Prisoner Who Wore Glasses." *Students should explain parallels in South Africa's history and Head's story.*

DIG DEEPER

With the class, return to Question 10, Reread and Discuss. Have students share the results of their discussions.

ASK STUDENTS whether they were satisfied with the outcome of their small-group discussions. Have each group share their conclusions about why Head included Brille's flashback to his time with his wife and children. What textual evidence did students find to support their conclusions?

- Guide each group to share whether they came to a unanimous conclusion about how the flashback worked in the story. If not, have groups share the variety of conclusions that emerged from their discussion.

- Ask groups to share the textual evidence that seemed the most compelling. Did they find explicit textual evidence that showed a parallel between Brille's role with his family and his role within the prison?

- As a class, discuss how Brille's reflections on his family caused him to behave differently with Hannetjie by the end of the story. *Students should realize that his wish for his children to cooperate influenced his decision to stop going "to extremes" (line 142) with Hannetjie.*

ASK STUDENTS to return to their Short Response answer and revise it based on the class discussion.

The Bonds Between Us

COLLECTION 3

The Bonds Between Us

"The welfare of each of us is dependent fundamentally upon the welfare of all of us."

—Theodore Roosevelt

And of Clay Are We Created

Short Story by Isabel Allende

Why This Text

Students may have difficulty identifying the theme of a complex literary text. In this story, a journalist is deeply affected by the plight of a girl trapped by a mudslide. Watching it all from faraway is the narrator, of whom we know little except for her intimate relationship with the journalist. With the help of the close-reading questions, students will explore these relationships to make inferences about the story's theme and draw conclusions about the author's underlying message.

Background Have students read the background and information about Isabel Allende. Point out that Allende's uncle, Salvador Allende, was president of Chile when he was overthrown and assassinated in 1973. As a result of the political turmoil Allende, her husband, and their children fled to Venezuela, where they lived in exile. It was during this period that she began to write her first novel, *The House of the Spirits*, which was based on her own family and the politics of Chile.

AS YOU READ Ask students to pay attention to the way the author uses descriptive details and the interactions of the characters to reveal the story's underlying theme.

Common Core Support

- cite strong and thorough textual evidence
- determine a theme or central idea of a text
- analyze how complex characters develop over the course of a text, interact with other characters, and develop the theme

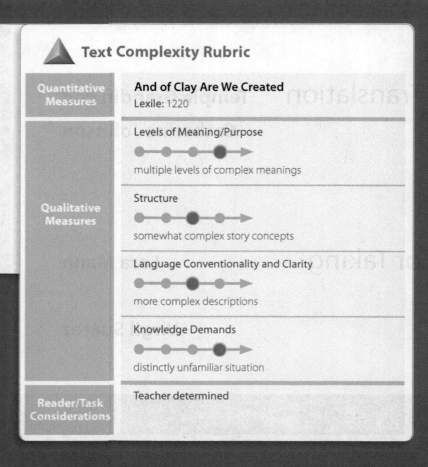

Text Complexity Rubric

Quantitative Measures	**And of Clay Are We Created** Lexile: 1220
Qualitative Measures	Levels of Meaning/Purpose — multiple levels of complex meanings
	Structure — somewhat complex story concepts
	Language Conventionality and Clarity — more complex descriptions
	Knowledge Demands — distinctly unfamiliar situation
Reader/Task Considerations	Teacher determined

Support Inferences About Theme

Students should read this story carefully all the way through. Close-reading questions at the bottom of the page will help them draw inferences about the story's theme. As they read, students should jot down comments or questions about the text in the margins.

WHEN STUDENTS STRUGGLE . . .

To help students determine the theme in "And of Clay Are We Created," have them work in small groups to fill out a chart like the one shown below.

CITE TEXT EVIDENCE For practice in analyzing how the author uses the characters to reveal the story's theme, ask students to find examples of each detail from the text listed in the chart below.

Details in the Text	Examples
Descriptive details about a character's appearance	"The president of the republic visited the area in his tailored safari jacket to confirm that this was the worst catastrophe of the century . . ." (lines 270–273) "She sank slowly, a flower in the mud." (line 317)
Character's words and actions	"I caught a glimpse of Rolf for a few seconds kneeling beside the mud pit. On the evening news broadcast, he was still in the same position . . ." (lines 286–288) "Rolf assured her that he loved her more than he could ever love anyone . . ." (lines 299–300)
Character's thoughts and observations	"He took excessive risks as an exercise of courage, training by day to conquer the monsters that tormented him by night." (lines 254–256) He was Azucena; he was buried in the clayey mud . . . (lines 257–258)
Symbols used to convey theme	"Your cameras lie forgotten in a closet . . ." (line 322) ". . . how they were freed from the clay, how they rose above the vultures and helicopters, . . . flew above the vast swamp of corruption and laments." (lines 306–308)

Background On November 13, 1985, the long-dormant Nevado del Ruiz volcano erupted in Colombia, South America. Molten rock and hot gases melted the volcano's thick ice cap and sent deadly mudslides down its slopes. More than 23,000 people died in the disaster—most of them in the town of Armero. The media focused a lot of attention on one thirteen-year-old girl named Omayra Sánchez who was trapped in the mud. **Isabel Allende** uses these facts as the basis for this work of fiction. In her story, the trapped girl is named Azucena, and the man who attempts to rescue her is journalist Rolf Carlé.

And of Clay Are We Created

Short Story by Isabel Allende

CLOSE READ
Notes

1. **READ ▶** As you read lines 1–30, begin to collect and cite evidence from the text.

- Circle the image that opens the story.
- In the margin, explain what the author foreshadows will happen to Carlé (lines 1–11).
- Underline text describing the consequences of the eruption.

They discovered the girl's head protruding from the mud pit, eyes wide open, calling soundlessly. She had a First Communion name, Azucena. Lily. In that vast cemetery where the odor of death was already attracting vultures from far away, and where the weeping of orphans and wails of the injured filled the air, the little girl obstinately clinging to life became the symbol of the tragedy. The television cameras transmitted so often the unbearable image of the head budding like a black squash from the clay that there was no one who did not recognize her and know her name. And every time we saw her on the screen, right behind her was Rolf Carlé, who had gone there on assignment, never suspecting that he would find a fragment of his past, lost thirty years before.

First a **subterranean** sob rocked the cotton fields, curling them like waves of foam. Geologists had set up their seismographs weeks before and knew that the mountain had awakened again. For some time they had

The author foreshadows that Carlé will find something from his past.

subterranean: *under the surface of the earth*

39

---

1. READ AND CITE TEXT EVIDENCE Remind students that symbols in a story often provide clues to the story's theme.

(A) ASK STUDENTS to note the frequent references to death in lines 1–11. How does this foreshadow what is to come? *It creates a sense of tragedy.* What do the vultures suggest? (line 4) *Vultures are attracted to the "odor of death"; we know there will be more deaths.*

Critical Vocabulary: subterranean (line 12) Have students share their definitions. Ask them what the phrase *subterranean sob* suggests. *It suggests that some dramatic activity is occurring beneath the earth's surface.*

predicted that the heat of the eruption could detach the eternal ice from the
slopes of the volcano, but no one heeded their warnings; they sounded like
the tales of frightened old women. The towns in the valley went about their
daily life, deaf to the moaning of the earth, until that fateful Wednesday
night in November when a prolonged roar announced the end of the world,
20 and walls of snow broke loose, rolling in an avalanche of clay, stones, and
water that descended on the villages and buried them beneath
unfathomable meters of telluric[1] vomit. As soon as the survivors emerged
from the paralysis of that first awful terror, they could see that houses,
plazas, churches, white cotton plantations, dark coffee forests, cattle
pastures—all had disappeared. Much later, after soldiers and volunteers had
arrived to rescue the living and try to assess the magnitude of the
cataclysm, it was calculated that beneath the mud lay more than twenty
thousand human beings and an indefinite number of animals putrefying in
a viscous soup. Forests and rivers had also been swept away, and there was
30 nothing to be seen but an immense desert of mire.

    When the station called before dawn, Rolf Carlé and I were together. I
crawled out of bed, dazed with sleep, and went to prepare coffee while he
hurriedly dressed. He stuffed his gear in the green canvas backpack he
always carried, and we said goodbye, as we had so many times before. I had
no **presentiments**. I sat in the kitchen, sipping my coffee and planning the
long hours without him, sure that he would be back the next day.

    He was one of the first to reach the scene, because while other reporters
were fighting their way to the edges of that morass in jeeps, bicycles, or on
foot, each getting there however he could, Rolf Carlé had the advantage of

[1] **telluric:** of or relating to the earth.

cataclysm:
*a violent and
destructive
natural event*

presentiment:
*a feeling that
something is
about to
happen*

(C)

---

2. **◀ REREAD** Reread lines 1–11. How does the narrator describe Carlé?
Make an inference about his character based on this and the description
of the devastation in lines 20–30. Cite text evidence in your response.

*The narrator describes Carlé as "right behind" Azucena every time
they saw him. Considering the extreme devastation of the town, you
can infer that Carlé is someone who shows strength and fortitude
amid danger and chaos.*

3. **READ ▶** As you read lines 31–65, continue to cite textual evidence.
  • Underline text that describes Carlé's job.
  • Circle the narrator's comments about how using a camera affects Carlé.

40

Armero, Colombia after the eruption of the Nevado del Ruiz volcano.

40 the television helicopter, which flew him over the avalanche. We watched
on our screens the footage captured by his assistant's camera, in which he
was up to his knees in muck, a microphone in his hand, in the midst of a
bedlam of lost children, wounded survivors, corpses, and devastation. The
story came to us in his calm voice. For years he had been a familiar figure
in newscasts, reporting live at the scene of battles and catastrophes with
awesome tenacity. Nothing could stop him, and I was always amazed at his
equanimity in the face of danger and suffering; it seemed as if nothing
could shake his fortitude or deter his curiosity. Fear seemed never to touch
him, although he had confessed to me that he was not a courageous man,
50 far from it. I believe that the lens of a camera had a strange effect on him; it
was as if it transported him to a different time from which he could watch
events without actually participating in them. When I knew him better, I
came to realize that this **fictive** distance seemed to protect him from his
own emotions.

(D)

equanimity:
*calmness,
composure*

fictive:
*not genuine;
feigned*

---

4. **◀ REREAD** Reread lines 31–54. Summarize what you know about the
narrator and her relationship with Carlé. What can you infer about their
emotional connection? Support your answer with textual evidence.

*The narrator is Carlé's wife or girlfriend. She misses him ("long hours
without him"). From her comment about protecting him from his
feelings, we can tell that she knows him intimately. She also indicates
how things between them have changed over time by saying, "When
I knew him better." He seems removed from his emotions, but she
seems to know what he is feeling.*

41

---

2. **REREAD AND CITE TEXT EVIDENCE**

(B) **ASK STUDENTS** to tell what they know about Rolf Carlé so
far. *We know Carlé is a reporter on assignment who will rediscover
his past (lines 8–11).* What do they know about the narrator? *Lines
8–9 tell us that the narrator is watching Rolf on TV; the narrator
admires him and is proud of him.*

3. **READ AND CITE TEXT EVIDENCE**

(C) **ASK STUDENTS** to cite evidence from the text that
indicates Rolf's job. *Lines 37–40 explicitly refer to him as a reporter
in "the television helicoper."*

Critical Vocabulary: cataclysm (line 27) Have students
explain the meaning of *cataclysm*. What kinds of cataclysms
have they seen covered on the news?

Critical Vocabulary: presentiment (line 35) Have students
share their definitions.

4. **REREAD AND CITE TEXT EVIDENCE** In these lines we learn
more about the narrator's connection to Rolf.

(D) **ASK STUDENTS** to revisit the line "and we said goodbye, as
we had so many times before" (line 34). What does this say about
the couple's relationship? *They had been together for a while; his
leaving to cover a big story was routine; she understood the nature of
his work.*

Critical Vocabulary: equanimity (line 47) Have students
explain the meaning of *equanimity*. Who can they think of that
has demonstrated "equanimity in the face of danger"?

Critical Vocabulary: fictive (line 53) Have students explain the
meaning of *fictive*, and ask them how Rolf's "fictive distance"
might help him in his chosen line of work. *It helps him cope with
the horror he regularly witnesses.*

Rolf Carlé was in on the story of Azucena from the beginning. He filmed the volunteers who discovered her, and the first persons who tried to reach her; his camera zoomed in on the girl, her dark face, her large desolate eyes, the plastered-down tangle of her hair. The mud was like quicksand around her, and anyone attempting to reach her was in danger of sinking.
60 They threw a rope to her that she made no effort to grasp until they shouted to her to catch it; then she pulled a hand from the mire and tried to move but immediately sank a little deeper. Rolf threw down his knapsack and the rest of his equipment and waded into the quagmire, commenting for his assistant's microphone that it was cold and that one could begin to smell the stench of corpses.

"What's your name?" he asked the girl, and she told him her flower name. "Don't move, Azucena," Rolf Carlé directed, and kept talking to her, without a thought for what he was saying, just to distract her, while slowly he worked his way forward in mud up to his waist. The air around him
70 seemed as murky as the mud.

It was impossible to reach her from the approach he was attempting, so he retreated and circled around where there seemed to be firmer footing. When finally he was close enough, he took the rope and tied it beneath her arms, so they could pull her out. He smiled at her with that smile that crinkles his eyes and makes him look like a little boy; he told her that everything was fine, that he was here with her now, that soon they would have her out. He signaled the others to pull, but as soon as the cord tensed, the girl screamed. They tried again, and her shoulders and arms appeared, but they could move her no farther; she was trapped. Someone suggested
80 that her legs might be caught in the collapsed walls of her house, but she said it was not just rubble, that she was also held by the bodies of her brothers and sisters clinging to her legs.

Carlé is determined to save the girl, but frustrated and heartbroken by his failed attempts.

5. **READ ▶** As you read lines 66–129, continue to cite textual evidence.
   • Underline the actions Carlé undertakes to help Azucena.
   • Circle text describing Carlé's attempt to get the pump and what he envisions will happen once it arrives.
   • In the margin, make an inference about how Carlé feels as he tries to rescue Azucena (lines 71–82).

42

"Don't worry, we'll get you out of here," Rolf promised. Despite the quality of the transmission, I could hear his voice break, and I loved him more than ever. Azucena looked at him but said nothing.

During those first hours Rolf Carlé exhausted all the resources of his **ingenuity** to rescue her. He struggled with poles and ropes, but every tug was an intolerable torture for the imprisoned girl. It occurred to him to use one of the poles as a lever but got no result and had to abandon the idea. He
90 talked a couple of soldiers into working with him for a while, but they had to leave because so many other victims were calling for help. The girl could not move, she barely could breathe, but she did not seem desperate, as if an ancestral resignation allowed her to accept her fate. The reporter, on the other hand, was determined to snatch her from death. Someone brought him a tire, which he placed beneath her arms like a life buoy, and then laid a plank near the hole to hold his weight and allow him to stay closer to her. As it was impossible to remove the rubble blindly, he tried once or twice to dive toward her feet but emerged frustrated, covered with mud, and spitting gravel. He concluded that he would have to have a pump to drain the water,
100 and radioed a request for one but received in return a message that there was no available transport and it could not be sent until the next morning.

"We can't wait that long!" Rolf Carlé shouted, but in the pandemonium no one stopped to **commiserate**. Many more hours would go by before he accepted that time had stagnated and reality had been irreparably distorted.

A military doctor came to examine the girl and observed that her heart was functioning well and that if she did not get too cold she could survive the night.

"Hang on, Azucena, we'll have the pump tomorrow," Rolf Carlé tried to console her.
110 "Don't leave me alone," she begged.

"No, of course I won't leave you."

Someone brought him coffee, and he helped the girl drink it, sip by sip. The warm liquid revived her, and she began telling him about her small life, about her family and her school, about how things were in that little bit of world before the volcano erupted. She was thirteen, and she had never been outside her village. Rolf Carlé, buoyed by a premature optimism, was convinced that everything would end well: the pump would arrive, they would drain the water, move the rubble, and Azucena would be transported by helicopter to a hospital where she would recover rapidly and where he
120 could visit her and bring her gifts. He thought, She's already too old for dolls, and I don't know what would please her; maybe a dress. I don't know

ingenuity:
cleverness in discovering, inventing, or planning

commiserate:
to feel or express sorrow or sympathy

43

---

5. **READ AND CITE TEXT EVIDENCE** In this section of text the narrator watches Rolf work to save Azucena's life. In lines 84–85 the narrator tells us that she "loved him more than ever."

E ASK STUDENTS to explain the narrator's comment. What does Rolf do that affects the narrator so much? *Although his words are encouraging, she can hear his voice break: he is pretending to be strong for the sake of the girl.*

Critical Vocabulary: ingenuity (line 87) Have students explain the meaning of *ingenuity*. Ask them why it took ingenuity to free Azucena. *The rescue workers couldn't pull her out without hurting her; they had to think of other ways to get her free.*

Critical Vocabulary: commiserate (line 103) Have students explain the meaning of *commiserate*. Why did no one stop to commiserate? *The pandemonium prevented people from stopping to react.*

FOR ELL STUDENTS Point to the verb *buoyed* (line 116). Explain, or ask a volunteer to explain, what a buoy is. (Many Spanish speakers might recognize its cognate, *boya*). Then ask another volunteer to guess or explain what the phrase *buoyed by a premature optimism* means. *supported by an unwarranted hopefulness*

much about women, he concluded, amused, reflecting that although he had
known many women in his lifetime, none had taught him these details. To
pass the hours he began to tell Azucena about his travels and adventures as
a news hound, and when he exhausted his memory, he called upon
imagination, inventing things he thought might entertain her. From time to
time she dozed, but he kept talking in the darkness, to assure her that he
was still there and to overcome the menace of uncertainty.

That was a long night.

130   Many miles away, I watched Rolf Carlé and the girl on a television
screen. I could not bear the wait at home, so I went to National Television,
where I often spent entire nights with Rolf editing programs. There, I was
near his world, and I could at least get a feeling of what he lived through
during those three decisive days. I called all the important people in the
city, senators, commanders of the armed forces, the North American
ambassador, and the president of National Petroleum, begging them for a
pump to remove the silt, but obtained only vague promises. I began to ask
for urgent help on radio and television, to see if there wasn't *someone* who
could help us. Between calls I would run to the newsroom to monitor the
140   satellite transmissions that periodically brought new details of the
catastrophe. While reporters selected scenes with most impact for the news
report, I searched for footage that featured Azucena's mud pit. The screen
reduced the disaster to a single plane and accentuated the tremendous
distance that separated me from Rolf Carlé; nonetheless, I was there with

---

6. **◀ REREAD**   Reread lines 86–129. What do you learn about Rolf and
Azucena in these lines? What do the last two sentences suggest about
Rolf's character?

Azucena is thirteen and has not traveled outside of her town. She's
scared to be alone. The last two sentences suggest that Rolf is
protective and strong, with great emotional and physical endurance.

---

7. **READ ▶**   As you read lines 130–207, continue to cite textual evidence.

- Underline text explaining how the narrator tries to feel close to Carlé.
- Circle text describing how Carlé tried to help Azucena.
- In the margin, explain what the narrator means when she says Carlé "had
  completely forgotten the camera" (lines 174–175).

44

> *The child's every suffering*
> *hurt me as it did him; I felt*
> *his frustration, his*
> *impotence.*

him. The child's every suffering hurt me as it did him; I felt his frustration,
his impotence. Faced with the impossibility of communicating with him,
the fantastic idea came to me that if I tried, I could reach him by force of
mind and in that way give him encouragement. I concentrated until I was
dizzy—a frenzied and futile activity. At times I would be overcome with
150   compassion and burst out crying; at other times, I was so drained I felt as if
I were staring through a telescope at the light of a star dead for a million
years.

I watched that hell on the first morning broadcast, cadavers of people
and animals awash in the current of new rivers formed overnight from the
melted snow. Above the mud rose the tops of trees and the bell towers of a
church where several people had taken refuge and were patiently awaiting
rescue teams. Hundreds of soldiers and volunteers from the civil defense
were clawing through rubble searching for survivors, while long rows of
ragged specters awaited their turn for a cup of hot broth. Radio networks
160   announced that their phones were jammed with calls from families offering
shelter to orphaned children. Drinking water was in scarce supply, along
with gasoline and food. Doctors, resigned to amputating arms and legs
without anesthesia, pled that at least they be sent serum and painkillers and
antibiotics; most of the roads, however, were impassable, and worse were the
bureaucratic obstacles that stood in the way. To top it all, the clay
contaminated by decomposing bodies threatened the living with an
outbreak of epidemics.

Azucena was shivering inside the tire that held her above the surface.
Immobility and tension had greatly weakened her, but she was conscious
170   and could still be heard when a microphone was held out to her. Her tone
was humble, as if apologizing for all the fuss. Rolf Carlé had a growth of
beard, and dark circles beneath his eyes; he looked near exhaustion. Even
from that enormous distance I could sense the quality of his weariness, so
different from the fatigue of other adventures. He had completely forgotten

bureaucratic:
governmental

45

---

6. **REREAD AND CITE TEXT EVIDENCE**   In lines 112–129, Rolf sits
by Azucena and they talk through the night.

F   ASK STUDENTS what Rolf's optimism conveys about him.
He is thinking positively, and imagining what he will buy for Azucena
when she is out. He may be used to things working out the way he
wants.

7. **READ AND CITE TEXT EVIDENCE**

G   ASK STUDENTS to revisit lines 50–54, in which the narrator
explains why the camera is so important to Rolf. In light of this,
have students consider why his forgetting about it is equally
important (lines 174–175). *We know that the camera "protects him*
from his emotions." Now Rolf is willing to feel emotions he had
suppressed.

Critical Vocabulary: bureaucratic   (line 165) Have students
share definitions of *bureaucratic*. Why might someone have
trouble because of "bureaucratic obstacles" standing in the
way? *Students may suggest having trouble reaching a politician on*
the phone or lodging a complaint against a big company.

FOR ELL STUDENTS   Point to the verb *clawing* (line 158).
Explain, or ask a volunteer to explain, what a claw is. Then ask
another volunteer to explain what the phrase *clawing through*
rubble means. *"scrabbling through the destruction"*

The search for victims and survivors continues in Guayabal, Colombia after the eruption of the Nevado del Ruiz volcano (November 16, 1985).

Carlé is face-to-face with Azucena and not looking at her through his camera.

the camera; he could not look at the girl through a lens any longer. The pictures we were receiving were not his assistant's but those of other reporters who had appropriated Azucena, bestowing on her the pathetic responsibility of embodying the horror of what had happened in that place. With the first light Rolf tried again to dislodge the obstacles that held the girl in her tomb, but he had only his hands to work with; he did not dare use a tool for fear of injuring her. He fed Azucena a cup of the cornmeal mush and bananas the army was distributing, but she immediately vomited it up. A doctor stated that she had a fever but added that there was little he could do: antibiotics were being reserved for cases of gangrene. A priest also passed by and blessed her, hanging a medal of the Virgin around her neck. By evening a gentle, persistent drizzle began to fall.

"The sky is weeping," Azucena murmured, and she, too, began to cry.

"Don't be afraid," Rolf begged. "You have to keep your strength up and be calm. Everything will be fine. I'm with you, and I'll get you out somehow."

Reporters returned to photograph Azucena and ask her the same questions, which she no longer tried to answer. In the meanwhile, more television and movie teams arrived with spools of cable, tapes, film, videos, precision lenses, recorders, sound consoles, lights, reflecting screens,

auxiliary motors, cartons of supplies, electricians, sound technicians, and cameramen: Azucena's face was beamed to millions of screens around the world. And all the while Rolf Carlé kept pleading for a pump. The improved technical facilities bore results, and National Television began receiving sharper pictures and clearer sound, the distance seemed suddenly compressed, and I had the horrible sensation that Azucena and Rolf were by my side, separated from me by impenetrable glass. I was able to follow events hour by hour; I knew everything my love did to wrest the girl from her prison and help her endure her suffering; I overheard fragments of what they said to one another and could guess the rest; I was present when she taught Rolf to pray and when he distracted her with the stories I had told him in a thousand and one nights beneath the white mosquito netting of our bed.

When darkness came on the second day, Rolf tried to sing Azucena to sleep with old Austrian folk songs he had learned from his mother, but she was far beyond sleep. They spent most of the night talking, each in a stupor of exhaustion and hunger and shaking with cold. That night, imperceptibly, the unyielding floodgates that had contained Rolf Carlé's past for so many years began to open, and the torrent of all that had lain hidden in the deepest and most secret layers of memory poured out, leveling before it the obstacles that had blocked his consciousness for so long. He could not tell it all to Azucena; she perhaps did not know there was a world beyond the sea or time previous to her own; she was not capable of imagining Europe in

The narrator explains how, through television and other media, she was able to follow Azucena and Carlé, to the point where she felt they "were by my side" but "separated by impenetrable glass."

8. **◀ REREAD** Reread lines 191–207. In the margin, explain what the narrator says about television and intimacy. In what way is it ironic that the improved transmission equipment makes it to the scene while the pump remains unobtainable?

It is ironic that modern equipment is brought in to transmit Azucena's nightmare to the homes and hearts of television viewers, while the simple machine, the pump that would remove the cause of her suffering, is not available.

9. **READ ▶** As you read lines 208–268, continue to cite textual evidence.

- In the margin, explain what you learn about Carlé's past (lines 217–224 and lines 232–248).
- Circle text explaining why Carlé feels he must confront his own fears.
- Underline what Rolf learns about why he takes risks.

8. **REREAD AND CITE TEXT EVIDENCE** In lines 200–201, the narrator tells us that the quality of the technology creates the sense that Rolf and Azucena are right there with her.

H ASK STUDENTS how this might affect the narrator emotionally. *She feels the horror more acutely; at the same time she feels she's listening in on a private conversation.*

9. **READ AND CITE TEXT EVIDENCE** Point out that in this section Rolf is suddenly overcome by long-repressed memories.

I ASK STUDENTS to explain why Rolf starts thinking about the past. *Rolf sings to Azucena songs his mother sang to him.* What effect does this have on him? *Trying to "mother" the girl in her last hours of life opens up locked memories and a floodgate of emotions.*

CLOSE READ
Notes

He'd had terrible experiences during WW II.

visceral:

felt deeply, profound

J

His father was cruel and abusive. He had a "sweet, retarded" sister who his father was ashamed of.

the years of the war. So he could not tell her of defeat, nor of the afternoon the Russians had led them to the concentration camp to bury prisoners
220 dead from starvation. Why should he describe to her how the naked bodies piled like a mountain of firewood resembled fragile china? How could he tell this dying child about ovens and gallows? Nor did he mention the night that he had seen his mother naked, shod in stiletto-heeled red boots, sobbing with humiliation. There was much he did not tell, but in those hours he relived for the first time all the things his mind had tried to erase. Azucena had surrendered her fear to him and so, without wishing it, had obliged Rolf to confront his own. There, beside that hellhole of mud, it was impossible for Rolf to flee from himself any longer, and the **visceral** terror he had lived as a boy suddenly invaded him. He reverted to the years when
230 he was the age of Azucena and younger, and, like her, found himself trapped in a pit without escape, buried in life, his head barely above ground; he saw before his eyes the boots and legs of his father, who had removed his belt and was whipping it in the air with the never-forgotten hiss of a viper coiled to strike. Sorrow flooded through him, intact and precise, as if it had lain always in his mind, waiting. He was once again in the armoire where his father locked him to punish him for imagined misbehavior, there where for eternal hours he had crouched with his eyes closed, not to see the darkness, with his hands over his ears to shut out the beating of his heart, trembling, huddled like a cornered animal. Wandering in the mist of his memories he
240 found his sister, Katharina, a sweet, retarded child who spent her life hiding, with the hope that her father would forget the disgrace of her having been born. With Katharina, Rolf crawled beneath the dining room table, and with her hid there under the long white tablecloth, two children forever embraced, alert to footsteps and voices. Katharina's scent melded with his own sweat, with aromas of cooking, garlic, soup, freshly baked bread, and the unexpected odor of putrescent clay. His sister's hand in his, her frightened breathing, her silk hair against his cheek, the candid gaze of her eyes. Katharina . . . Katharina materialized before him, floating on the air like a flag, clothed in the white tablecloth, now a winding sheet, and at last
250 he could weep for her death and for the guilt of having abandoned her. He understood then that all his exploits as a reporter, the feats that had won him such recognition and fame, were merely an attempt to keep his most ancient fears at bay, a stratagem for taking refuge behind a lens to test whether reality was more tolerable from that perspective. He took excessive risks as an exercise of courage, training by day to conquer the monsters that tormented him by night. But he had to come face to face with the moment of truth; he could not continue to escape his past. He was Azucena; he was buried in the clayey mud; his terror was not the distant emotion of an almost forgotten childhood, it was a claw sunk in his throat. In the flush of

48

his tears he saw his mother, dressed in black and clutching her imitation-
260 crocodile pocketbook to her bosom, just as he had last seen her on the dock when she had come to put him on the boat to South America. She had not come to dry his tears, but to tell him to pick up a shovel: the war was over and now they must bury the dead.

"Don't cry. I don't hurt anymore. I'm fine," Azucena said when dawn came.

"I'm not crying for you," Rolf Carlé smiled. "I'm crying for myself. I hurt all over."

The third day in the valley of the cataclysm began with a pale light filtering through storm clouds. The president of the republic visited the area
270 in his tailored safari jacket to confirm that this was the worst catastrophe of the century; the country was in mourning; sister nations had offered aid; he had ordered a state of siege; the armed forces would be merciless; anyone caught stealing or committing other offenses would be shot on sight. He added that it was impossible to remove all the corpses or count the thousands who had disappeared; the entire valley would be declared holy ground, and bishops would come to celebrate a solemn mass for the souls of the victims. He went to the army field tents to offer relief in the form of vague promises to crowds of the rescued, then to the improvised hospital to

K

---

10. ◀ REREAD Reread lines 208–268. In what way is Carlé's interaction with Azucena changing him?

Rolf's interaction with Azucena is making him face painful memories he has long ago buried. Just as Azucena is buried in mud, Carlé is buried in the horrors of his traumatic childhood. He realizes he has pushed himself in his career to keep "his most ancient fears at bay." He sees now that "he could not continue to escape his past."

---

11. READ ▶ As you read lines 269–310, continue to cite textual evidence.

• Circle adjectives the narrator uses that indicate her feelings about the president and his actions.
• Underline text that describes the interactions between Carlé and Azucena.

49

Critical Vocabulary: visceral (line 228) Have students share definitions of *visceral*. What is a visceral understanding? *It's something that is understood instinctively.*

10. REREAD AND CITE TEXT EVIDENCE

J **ASK STUDENTS** what in Rolf's background makes him identify so completely with Azucena. How do their situations mirror each other? *Both have known terror; both have been forsaken by those who should have been protecting them; like Azucena, Rolf is "trapped in a pit without escape, buried in life . . ." (lines 230–231).*

11. READ AND CITE TEXT EVIDENCE

K **ASK STUDENTS** to analyze the president's proposals for dealing with the crisis. How does his language show he is removed from the actual situation? *The president talks in grandiose, bureaucratic, abstract terms: "worst catastrophe of the century"; "sister nations"; "state of siege"; "armed forces; "all the corpses" (lines 271–275).*

FOR ELL STUDENTS Explain that a *state of siege* (*estado de sitio,* in Spanish) is a situation in which police or soldiers take control of a city or of a whole country.

The town of Armero, Colombia, submerged by floods after the Nevado del Ruiz volcano erupted (November, 18, 1985).

The president's "tailored safari jacket" and "limp statesman's hand" suggest that he is putting on a show rather than providing substantive relief.

280 offer a word of encouragement to doctors and nurses worn down from so many hours of tribulations. Then he asked to be taken to see Azucena, the little girl the whole world had seen. He waved to her with a limp statesman's hand, and microphones recorded his emotional voice and paternal tone as he told her that her courage had served as an example to the nation. Rolf Carlé interrupted to ask for a pump, and the president assured him that he personally would attend to the matter. I caught a glimpse of Rolf for a few seconds kneeling beside the mud pit. On the evening news broadcast, he was still in the same position; and I, glued to the screen like a fortune teller to her crystal ball, could tell that something fundamental had changed in

290 him. I knew somehow that during the night his defenses had crumbled and he had given in to grief; finally he was vulnerable. The girl had touched a part of him that he himself had no access to, a part he had never shared with me. Rolf had wanted to console her, but it was Azucena who had given him consolation.

I recognized the precise moment at which Rolf gave up the fight and surrendered to the torture of watching the girl die. I was with them, three days and two nights, spying on them from the other side of life. I was there when she told him that in all her thirteen years no boy had ever loved her and that it was a pity to leave this world without knowing love. Rolf assured

300 her that he loved her more than he could ever love anyone, more than he loved his mother, more than his sister, more than all the women who had slept in his arms, more than he loved me, his life companion, who would have given anything to be trapped in that well in her place, who would have exchanged her life for Azucena's, and I watched as he leaned down to kiss her poor forehead, consumed by a sweet, sad emotion he could not name. I felt how in that instant both were saved from despair, how they were freed from the clay, how they rose above the vultures and helicopters, how together they flew above the vast swamp of corruption and laments. How, finally, they were able to accept death. Rolf Carlé prayed in silence that she

310 would die quickly, because such pain cannot be borne.

By then I had obtained a pump and was in touch with a general who had agreed to ship it the next morning on a military cargo plane. But on the night of that third day, beneath the unblinking focus of quartz lamps and the lens of a hundred cameras, Azucena gave up, her eyes locked with those of the friend who had sustained her to the end. Rolf Carlé removed the life buoy, closed her eyelids, held her to his chest for a few moments, and then let her go. She sank slowly, a flower in the mud.

 You are back with me, but you are not the same man. I often accompany you to the station, and we watch the videos of Azucena again;

12. ◀ REREAD Reread lines 269–286. In the margin, make an inference about how the narrator feels about the president's visit. Support your answer with explicit textual evidence.

13. READ ▶ As you read lines 311–326, continue to cite textual evidence.
• Underline text that describes what happens between Carlé and Azucena.
• Circle text describing how Carlé is no longer the person he used to be.

---

12. REREAD AND CITE TEXT EVIDENCE

L ASK STUDENTS to describe what the president does when he meets Azucena for the first time. *He "waved to her with a limp statesman's hand" (lines 282–283).* What has Rolf been doing in the meantime? *Rolf "interrupted to ask for a pump" as he is "kneeling beside the mud pit" (lines 284–287).*

13. READ AND CITE TEXT EVIDENCE   Point out that although Rolf is no longer the man he used to be, the narrator is hopeful about their future together.

M ASK STUDENTS to cite evidence showing that the narrator will not abandon Rolf. *She accompanies him to the station and they watch videos of Azucena together; she says she will wait for him to "complete the voyage" into himself and then they will "walk hand in hand, as before" (lines 318–326).*

FOR ELL STUDENTS Explain that *well* is often used as an adverb, but it can also be a noun that means "a deep hole from which water can be removed." In line 303, point out the adjective *that* before *well*. Explain that an adjective is usually followed by a noun, so in this context the meaning of *well* is "a place with water."

320   you study them intently, looking for something you could have done to save her, something you did not think of in time. Or maybe you study them to see yourself as if in a mirror, naked. Your cameras lie forgotten in a closet; you do not write or sing; you sit long hours before the window, staring at the mountains. Beside you, I wait for you to complete the voyage into yourself, for the old wounds to heal. I know that when you return from your nightmares, we shall again walk hand in hand, as before.

14. ◀ **REREAD AND DISCUSS**   Reread lines 318–326. With a small group, discuss the author's switch to second person point of view in these lines. Why does she do this, and what effect does it have on you as a reader?

SHORT RESPONSE

Cite Text Evidence   What is a theme of the story? Review your reading notes and **cite text evidence** to support your answer.

This selection has several themes. One of the themes is "The technology of modern life both brings us together and keeps us apart." We are told a story of immense human suffering through the eyes of a narrator who views it on television. The media industry is portrayed as distancing and isolating but also allowing us to participate vicariously in human experience. Through the media we can observe a lot, but always at a distance. Another theme is "Human connection has the potential for healing lives." The theme is supported by the change that occurs within Carlé, who through his profound connection with Azucena begins to heal his own long-buried wounds.

52

TO CHALLENGE STUDENTS . . .

To give students a real-life context for Allende's story, tell them that it is based on an actual event: the 1985 eruption of the Nevado del Ruiz volcano in Colombia, South America, which caused an estimated 23,000 deaths and destroyed some villages. The character of Azucena was based on a 13-year-old girl named Omayra Sánchez. Like the fictional Azucena, Omayra was trapped beneath the debris of her home for three days while the world watched. Her death from exposure highlighted the failure of officials to respond to the disaster by providing much-needed supplies and equipment.

ASK STUDENTS to research the real story of Omayra Sánchez. Have groups collect newspaper and magazine articles about her death and the public outcry that followed. Each group can research a different aspect of the story or report on it from a different point of view.

Students might examine how the government received warnings from multiple organizations when volcanic activity was first detected earlier that year; and yet, preparedness measures were not in place when the eruption took place. Students can compare Nevado del Ruiz to other well-known volcanoes, for instance, the eruption of Mount St. Helens in Washington state in 1980 (and more recently, in 2005).

After students have completed their research, they can do a point-by-point analysis comparing the fictional and historical versions of the catastrophe in Colombia. Have them discuss why Allende might have wanted to change certain details of the story.

---

14. **REREAD AND DISCUSS USING TEXT EVIDENCE**   Point out that for most of the story, the narrator is speaking in the first person, but in the last paragraph she switches point of view.

 ASK STUDENTS to analyze the last paragraph. Who is the "you" the narrator refers to? *The "you" is Rolf.* How does this change in point of view affect the story? *The narrator is talking directly to Rolf, almost as if the readers are out of the picture.*

SHORT RESPONSE

Cite Text Evidence   Students' responses should include text evidence that supports their positions. They should:

- make inferences about the story's theme.
- analyze characters based on their interactions.
- interpret symbols that convey the story's theme.

DIG DEEPER

With the class, return to Question 3, Read. Have students share their responses.

ASK STUDENTS to think about the theme of "fictive distance" in this story.

- Students can provide text evidence showing how technology (i.e., the camera lens, the TV screen) separates people from each other and limits their capacity for empathy.
- Students can explore how the theme of "distance" runs through the story. How is this theme reflected in the relationships between the narrator and Rolf, the narrator and Azucena, and Rolf and Azucena? How does it play out in the actions of the president? How is Rolf's character shaped by his need for distance and his rejection of it?

ASK STUDENTS to return to Question 7, Read. Have students share their responses.

- Have students cite evidence of Rolf's state of mind at the point in the story where he "forgets" about his camera. What do they know about him that might explain his behavior?
- Students may point out Rolf's need to distance himself from his own past. Why might he have needed to create distance?
- Have students think about how well the camera worked for the narrator. How did it serve her interests?

ASK STUDENTS to return to Question 14, Reread and Discuss. Have students discuss their responses.

- Have students cite evidence showing how the author uses character, tone, and point of view to address the theme of "distance."
- Compare the narrator's tone in the last paragraph to the tone of the rest of the story. Which tone is the more distant?
- Have students analyze why the narrator switches from first-person to second-person point of view. What does it say about the narrator's distance from Rolf? What does it say about the author's distance from her subject?

CLOSE READING NOTES

_____

_____

_____

_____

_____

_____

_____

_____

_____

_____

_____

_____

_____

_____

_____

_____

_____

_____

_____

_____

_____

_____

_____

_____

_____

_____

_____

_____

_____

_____

_____

from Animals in Translation

Science Writing by Temple Grandin and Catherine Johnson

Why This Text

Students may have difficulty evaluating an argument if they don't understand the author's claims. Arguments such as this one by Temple Grandin and Catherine Johnson may have difficult technical language or complex reasoning that becomes clear only with careful study. With the help of the close-reading questions, students will analyze the development and refinement of the author's claim about the abilities of animals.

Background Have students read the background information about Temple Grandin, an accomplished adult with autism, who is a doctor of animal science, a best-selling author, and a leader in the autism advocacy movement. Introduce the selection by telling students that Grandin believes in the extraordinary ability of animals to perceive the world around them. An expert in animal behavior, one of her recent books—*Animals Make Us Human: Creating the Best Life for Animals*—focuses on the emotional lives of animals.

AS YOU READ Ask students to pay close attention to the reasons Grandin gives to support her claim that animals have "extreme perception." How soon into the selection can students begin to identify her position?

 Common Core Support

- cite multiple pieces of evidence
- determine the meaning of words and phrases as they are used in a text, including technical meanings
- analyze how an author's ideas and claims are developed and refined
- evaluate the argument and claims in a text, assessing whether the reasoning is valid and the evidence is sufficient

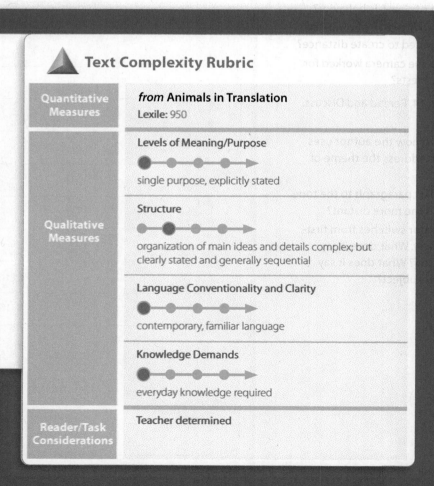

Text Complexity Rubric

Quantitative Measures

from **Animals in Translation**
Lexile: 950

Qualitative Measures

Levels of Meaning/Purpose

single purpose, explicitly stated

Structure

organization of main ideas and details complex; but clearly stated and generally sequential

Language Conventionality and Clarity

contemporary, familiar language

Knowledge Demands

everyday knowledge required

Reader/Task Considerations

Teacher determined

Analyze an Author's Claims

Students should read this scientific text carefully all the way through. Close-reading questions at the bottom of the page will help them focus on a thorough analysis of the author's claim as well as the counterclaim she cites. As they read, students should record comments or questions about the text in the side margins.

WHEN STUDENTS STRUGGLE . . .

To help students follow the reasons Grandin cites to support her claim, have students work in small groups to fill out a chart, such as the one shown below, as they analyze this scientific text.

CITE TEXT EVIDENCE For practice in analyzing an argument, ask students to cite the evidence that Grandin gives to support her claim.

CLAIM: *Animals have astonishing abilities to sense things around them.*

SUPPORT:

Reason 1: *Compared to humans, animals have "extreme perception."*

Reason 2: *Animals do not have extrasensory perception (ESP); they have a "supersensitive sensory apparatus."*

Reason 3: *Jane's cat always knows when Jane is on her way home.*

Reason 4: *As a "visual thinker," Grandin is able to imagine how Jane's cat uses sound cues to sense Jane's arrival.*

Background *One of the world's most accomplished adults with autism,* **Temple Grandin** *is a professor at Colorado State University. She is also the author of several best-selling books, including* Animals In Translation *from which this excerpt is taken. Drawing upon her long career as an animal scientist and her own experiences with autism,* Animals in Translation *provides a unique message about the way animals act, think, and feel.* **Catherine Johnson,** *Grandin's coauthor, specializes in writing about the brain. She is also no stranger to autism—two of her sons are autistic.*

from
Animals in Translation

Science Writing by Temple Grandin and Catherine Johnson

CLOSE READ
Notes

1. **READ ▶** As you read lines 1–8, begin to collect and cite text evidence.
   - Underline the claim Grandin makes about animal perception in the first paragraph, and restate it in the margin.
   - Circle the sentence that explains what most people think about animals.
   - Underline Grandin's claim in the second paragraph.

Extreme Perception: The Mystery of Jane's Cat

Ⓐ Ⓑ Compared to humans, animals have astonishing abilities to perceive things in the world. They have *extreme perception*. Their sensory[1] worlds are so much richer than ours it's almost as if we're deaf and blind. That's probably why a lot of people think animals have ESP.[2] Animals have such incredible abilities to perceive things we can't that the only explanation we can come up with is extrasensory perception. There's even a scientist in England who's written books about animals having ESP. But they don't have ESP, they just have a supersensitive sensory apparatus.

Animals have far greater perception than that of humans.

[1] **sensory:** of or related to any of the five senses.
[2] **ESP:** an abbreviation for extrasensory perception, the act of perceiving or communicating by means other than the five senses.

53

---

1. **READ AND CITE TEXT EVIDENCE** Explain that Grandin opens with a blanket statement in which she claims that "Compared to humans, animals have astonishing abilities to perceive things in the world." This opening serves a dual purpose: it "grabs" the reader's attention and poses the topic this selection will argue.

Ⓐ **ASK STUDENTS** to determine how Grandin begins to address her argument (or claim) by citing specific textual evidence in lines 1–8. *Responses should include references to evidence in lines 1–3 and 8.*

FOR ELL STUDENTS Point out the word *supersensitive* in line 8. Explain that the prefix *super-* means "above" or "beyond," or "to a great degree." Elicit some simple words with this prefix, such as *superhighway* or *supercomputer*, defining each word. Tell students that words with this prefix are often a part of technical vocabulary.

Jane and her husband claim that her cat has ESP because it always knows when Jane comes home, no matter what time.

C

Take the cat who knows when its owner is coming home. My friend
10 Jane, who lives in a city apartment, has a cat who always knows when she's
on her way home. Jane's husband works at home, and five minutes before
Jane comes home he'll see the cat go to the door, sit down, and wait. Since
Jane doesn't come home at the same time every day, the cat isn't going by its
sense of time, although animals also have an incredible sense of time.
Sigmund Freud³ used to have his dog with him every time he saw a patient,
and he never had to look at his watch to tell when the session was over. The
dog always let him know. Parents tell me autistic kids do the same thing.
The only explanation Jane and her husband could come up with was ESP.
The cat must have been picking up Jane's I'm-coming-home-now thoughts.

20 Jane asked me to figure out how her cat could predict her arrival. Since
I've never seen Jane's apartment I used my mother's New York City
apartment as a model for solving the mystery. In my imagination I watched
my mother's gray Persian cat walk around the apartment and look out the

³ **Sigmund Freud:** Austrian founder of psychoanalysis whose theories significantly influenced modern thought.

2. ◀ REREAD Reread lines 1–8. In your own words, explain the claim that Grandin makes about animals and ESP. What analogy does she make to get across her point about animals' "abilities to perceive the world"? Support your answer with explicit textual evidence.

Grandin claims that animals have astonishing abilities to sense things around them. She likens the difference in human and animal perceptions to the difference between a deaf and blind person to one with hearing and sight. Rather than having "extra sensory" perception, Grandin claims animals have "super sensory" perception.

3. READ ▶ As you read lines 9–28, continue to cite textual evidence.
• Underline text describing the perceptive behavior of Jane's cat.
• Restate the claim that Jane and her husband make about her cat in the margin (lines 9–19).
• Circle the claim that Grandin gives to account for the cat's behavior, and restate it in the margin (lines 24–28).

54

" Jane finally gave me the crucial piece of information that solved the cat mystery . . . "

Grandin thinks that Jane's cat can see her somehow and recognizes her body language.

She uses "videos" in her mind to help her visualize how the cat was getting sound cues.

D

window. Possibly the cat could see Jane walking down the street. Even
though he would not be able to see Jane's face from the twelfth floor he
would probably be able to recognize her body language. Animals are very
sensitive to body language. The cat would probably be able to recognize
Jane's walk.

E F

30 Next I thought about sound cues. Since I am a visual thinker I used
"videos" in my imagination to move the cat around in the apartment to
determine how it could be getting sound cues that Jane would be arriving a
few minutes later. In my mind's eye I positioned the cat with its ear next to
the crack between the door and the door frame. I thought maybe he could
hear Jane's voice on the elevator. But as I played a tape of my mother getting
onto the elevator in the lobby, I realized that there would be many days
when Mother would ride the elevator alone and silent. She would speak on
the elevator for only some of the trips—when there were other people in the
elevator car with her—but not all of them.

40 So I asked Jane, "Is the cat always at the door, or is he at the door only
sometimes?"

She said the cat is always at the door.

That meant the cat had to be hearing Jane's voice on the elevator every
day. After I questioned her some more, Jane finally gave me the crucial
piece of information that solved the cat mystery: her building does not have
a push-button elevator. The elevator is operated by a person. So when Jane
got on the elevator she probably said "Hi" to the operator.

4. ◀ REREAD AND DISCUSS With a small group, discuss whether you believe Grandin's explanation for the cat's behavior in lines 24–28. Why or why not?

5. READ ▶ As you read lines 29–58, underline places in the text where Grandin refers to her experiences with autism.

55

---

2. REREAD AND CITE TEXT EVIDENCE Grandin counters the claim that assumes that animals possess extrasensory perception (ESP) by proposing that they have "a supersensitive sensory apparatus" instead.

B **ASK STUDENTS** why many people think animals have ESP. *Students should cite specific textual evidence from lines 1–8.*

3. READ AND CITE TEXT EVIDENCE

C **ASK STUDENTS** to read their margin notes to a partner and then write one response that best restates the opposing viewpoint stated by Jane and her husband about Jane's cat. *Students should cite specific evidence from the text in lines 18–19.*

4. REREAD AND DISCUSS USING TEXT EVIDENCE

D **ASK STUDENTS** to appoint a reporter for each group to cite specific textual evidence to support whether or not they agree with Grandin's explanation for Jane's cat's behavior. *Students should cite textual evidence from lines 24–28.*

5. READ AND CITE TEXT EVIDENCE Because Grandin is a "visual thinker," she is able to visualize how Jane's cat is acquiring sound cues to sense Jane's arrival.

E **ASK STUDENTS** to explain how Grandin uses her experience with autism to create "videos" in her mind to move the cat around Jane's apartment and to play a "tape" of her mother getting into her own elevator. *Grandin was able to visualize the cat in various locations and what it could hear there (lines 30–32). She imagined her mother in a similar situation riding an elevator (lines 34–36 and 48–51).*

She visualizes an elevator operator, and imagines Jane greeting him out loud.

A new image flashed into my head. I created an elevator with an operator for my mother's building. To make the image I used the same method people use in computer graphics. I pulled an image of my mother's
50   elevator out of memory and combined it with an image of the elevator operator I saw one time at the Ritz in Boston. He had white gloves and a black tuxedo. I lifted the brass elevator control panel and its tuxedoed operator from my Ritz memory file and placed them inside my mother's elevator.

That was the answer. The fact that Jane's building had an elevator operator provided the cat with the sound of Jane's voice while Jane was still down on the first floor. That's why the cat went to the door to wait. The cat wasn't predicting Jane's arrival; for the cat Jane was already home.

6. ◀ **REREAD**   As you reread lines 29–54, note in the margin how Grandin's experiences with autism led her to solve the mystery of Jane's cat.

SHORT RESPONSE

Cite Text Evidence   Did Grandin's story about Jane's cat convince you that animals have an amazing ability to perceive their world. Why or why not? Explain, **citing evidence from the text** in your response.

Possible response: It seems clear that animals have an incredible ability to perceive things that humans cannot, displaying a supersensitivity that some people, even scientists, have thought was ESP. Grandin's claim that animals do not have ESP—just a "supersensitive sensory apparatus"—is convincing and is supported by the evidence she offers concerning the behavior of Jane's cat. Although the cat's owners believe it has ESP, Grandin relies on scientific evidence and her own experiences to convince her readers that there is a reason behind animal perceptions, not just a magical sense.

56

6. **REREAD AND CITE TEXT EVIDENCE**

F   **ASK STUDENTS** to discuss the last clue that leads Grandin to solve the mystery of Jane's cat. *Students should recognize that Grandin realizes there is an elevator operator when she uses visual images from her memory. Students should cite evidence from lines 32–36 and 48–51.*

SHORT RESPONSE

Cite Text Evidence   Students should:

- explain whether or not Grandin convinced them of her argument.
- give reasons for their point of view.
- cite specific evidence from the text to support their reasons.

TO CHALLENGE STUDENTS . . .

For more context on the behavior of animals and our understanding of it, students can find out more about Temple Grandin's work.

ASK STUDENTS to read other excerpts from *Animals in Translation* or to research Temple Grandin in articles in print or online. Have students report their findings to the class.

- Aside from writing books, what does Grandin do? *She is Professor of Animal Science at Colorado State University. She is an advocate for people with autism, and for animal welfare. She is one of the world's few designers of equipment for handling livestock, and is a consultant to many large livestock companies.*

- What influence has Grandin had on people's understanding of animal behavior? *She has shown that animals experience emotions and pain. Her work improving slaughterhouse systems has resulted in a more humane ending to animals' lives, so much so that she has even received an award from PETA. She is revered by animal rights groups.*

DIG DEEPER

With the class, return to Question 4, Reread and Discuss. Have students share the results of their discussion.

ASK STUDENTS whether they were satisfied with the outcome of their small-group discussions. Have each group share whether or not they agreed with Grandin's explanation for Jane's cat's behavior. What compelling evidence did the groups cite from the selection to support their opinion?

- Encourage students to tell whether there was any convincing text evidence cited by group members holding a minority opinion. If so, why didn't it sway the group?

- Have groups explain how they decided whether or not Grandin's evidence was sufficient to support her findings. Did everyone in the group agree as to what made the evidence sufficient? How did the group resolve any conflicts or disagreements?

- After students have shared the results of their group's discussion, ask whether another group shared any findings they wished they had brought to the table.

ASK STUDENTS to return to their Short Response answer and revise it based on the class discussion.

Poems About Family

My Ceremony For Taking
Poem by Lara Mann

The Stayer
Poem by Virgil Suárez

Why These Texts

A poem often presents a lot of information in a small package. The two poems that students will read here are both very short, and the authors have chosen their words carefully to convey mood and meaning. With the help of the close-reading questions, students will analyze these word choices and interpret the figurative language in each poem. This close reading will help students analyze the impact of word choices on each poem's meaning and tone.

Background Have students read the background and discuss the Dylan Thomas quote. Then have them read the biographical information about Lara Mann and Virgil Suárez. Point out that both poets have had to balance the cultures that they have been part of. Ask students to predict what each poem might be about, based on the biographical information and the titles of the poems.

AS YOU READ Ask students to pay attention to the authors' word choices in each poem. In what ways do the words they choose help the author set the tone and mood and deepen the poem's meaning?

Common Core Support

- cite strong and thorough textual evidence
- interpret figurative language used in a text
- analyze the cumulative impact of specific word choices on meaning and tone

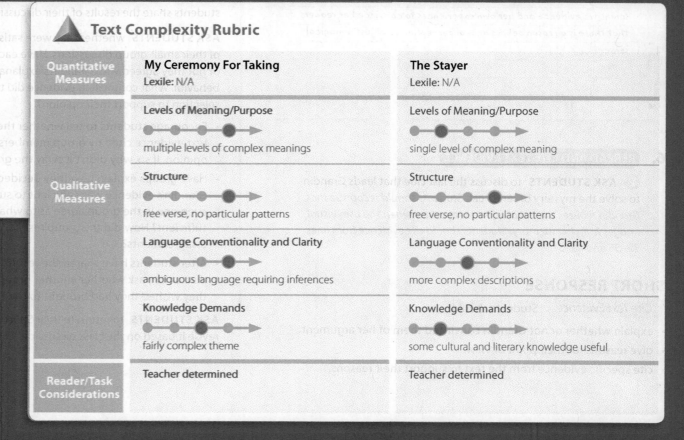

Text Complexity Rubric

	My Ceremony For Taking	The Stayer
Quantitative Measures	Lexile: N/A	Lexile: N/A
Qualitative Measures	**Levels of Meaning/Purpose** multiple levels of complex meanings	**Levels of Meaning/Purpose** single level of complex meaning
	Structure free verse, no particular patterns	**Structure** free verse, no particular patterns
	Language Conventionality and Clarity ambiguous language requiring inferences	**Language Conventionality and Clarity** more complex descriptions
	Knowledge Demands fairly complex theme	**Knowledge Demands** some cultural and literary knowledge useful
Reader/Task Considerations	Teacher determined	Teacher determined

Strategies for CLOSE READING

Interpret Figurative Language

Students should read these poems carefully all the way through. Close-reading questions at the bottom of the page will help them analyze the word choices the authors make. As they read, students should jot down comments or questions about the text in the margins.

WHEN STUDENTS STRUGGLE . . .

To help students analyze "My Ceremony For Taking" and "The Stayer," have them work in small groups to fill out a chart like the one shown below.

CITE TEXT EVIDENCE For practice in interpreting figurative language and its effects on a poem's tone, mood, and meaning, ask students to interpret text examples from the poems in the chart.

Words from the Poems	Interpretation
"burned my family's death scaffold"	utterly destroyed the family with finality
"birth dirt"	a small amount of dirt from the place where one was born
"a lock . . . pressed into the dirt I took for payment, to leave part of myself"	the speaker pulls out a lock of her hair and pushes it into the dirt she has taken
"light, the way it darted through holes in the tin roof"	beams of light shine through the holes in the roof
"motes danced in the shaft of white light"	The dust sparkled in the light in the shack.
"the meaning of stay"	Staying is more important than emptiness.

Background Poems about family often give us insights not only into the author's life and upbringing, but also into our own. As you read the two poems selected here, think of these lines written by the poet Dylan Thomas: "You can tear a poem apart to see what makes it tick . . . You're back with the mystery of having been moved by words. The best craftsmanship always leaves holes and gaps . . . so that something that is not in the poem can creep, crawl, flash or thunder in."

Poems About Family

My Ceremony For Taking	Lara Mann
The Stayer	Virgil Suárez

Lara Mann *was born in Kansas, and is a member of the Choctaw Nation of Oklahoma. She is of English, Irish, Choctaw, French, German, Scottish, Spanish, Cherokee, Welsh, and Mohawk descent. Common themes in her work include the integration of both Native American and American culture and exposing the inaccurate stereotypes that many Americans assign to Native Americans.*

Virgil Suárez *By the time Virgil Suárez was twelve years old, his family had moved across the ocean twice—first from Cuba to Spain and then from Spain to the United States. These childhood experiences continue to influence the predominant themes of Suárez's works— family ties, immigration, and exile. He draws upon his own memories of people and places for his work, and credits his family for providing him with such an interesting array of characters. He notes, "I write about my life, and my life informs my writing."*

1. **READ ▶** As you read lines 1–24, begin to collect and cite text evidence.

   • Underline words and phrases that have similar meanings.
   • Circle examples of figurative language.
   • In the margin, write your interpretation of lines 1–5.

My Ceremony For Taking
Lara Mann

The speaker doesn't know what to do now that her family has been ended by words of hurt.

Ⓐ No one told me how it should be, these steps
for taking. Some things I know without being told.
The words told to me ended my family,
the words I told burned my family's death scaffold;
5 those things we say when we are hurt, to hurt.

I wanted to take pieces of my ancestor's
homes with me, the way some homelands are sacred.
The way some carry their birth dirt for protection.
But these locations are revered, and for me,
10 the taking was blasphemous.

She feels split in half because her family is being torn apart.

Ⓑ My parents split, and I felt
absolutely halved, though what was left of me
was unclear. I needed a ceremony.
It had to require pain,
15 a sacrifice. It had to be missed.

That summer, when we went, my dad and I,
back to Alabama and Mississippi
to try to fix our **fissured** selves.
I pulled out hair many times.

fissure:
a narrow opening or a crack

20 Choctaws were known for hair: long, thick, honor-
banner. I gave of myself. My hair was my thanks;
parts of me pulled out, white-root waving; a lock,
not just a strand, pressed into the dirt I took
for payment, to leave part of myself.

2. **◀ REREAD** Reread lines 11–24 of "My Ceremony For Taking." In the margin, explain why the speaker feels "split."

58

---

3. **READ ▶** As you read lines 1–34 of "The Stayer," collect and cite text evidence.

   • Circle reasons for Chicho staying in Cuba.
   • In the margin, explain why Chicho is called "crazy."
   • Underline figurative language, or descriptive words, that create tone.

The Stayer
Virgil Suárez

Simply, my uncle Chicho stayed
back in Cuba, against the family's
advice, because everyone left

and he chose to stay, and this act
5 of staying marked him as "crazy"
with most of the men, and he stayed

there in a shack behind my aunt's
clapboard house, sat in the dark
of most days in the middle

He's called "crazy" because he stayed in Cuba when everyone else left.

10 of the packed-dirt floor and nodded
Ⓒ at the insistence of light, the way
it darted through holes in the tin

roof where the rain drummed
like the gallop of spooked horses.
15 This is where he was born, he chanted

Ⓓ under his breath to no one, why should
he leave, live in perpetual longing
within exile? He learned long ago

to count the passing of time
20 in how **motes** danced in the shaft
of white light, the *chicharras*[1] echoed

motes:
specks of dust

their trill against the emptiness
of life, against the wake of resistance
in this place he knew as a child,

[1] *chicharras*: cicadas, insects that produce a loud buzzing noise.

59

---

1. **READ AND CITE TEXT EVIDENCE** Tell students that lines 1–5 of "My Ceremony For Taking" define the situation in the poem.

   Ⓐ **ASK STUDENTS** what the speaker expresses in the first two lines. *She says that she knows what steps she will take, even though nobody told her.* What has happened? *She is told that her family is breaking up.*

2. **REREAD AND CITE TEXT EVIDENCE**

   Ⓑ **ASK STUDENTS** to cite text from lines 11–24 that refers to being "split." *Students should cite: "My parents split" (line 11); "I felt absolutely halved" (lines 11–12); "to fix our fissured selves" (line 18); "parts of me pulled out" (line 22).*

   Critical Vocabulary: fissure (line 18) Have students share their definitions of *fissure*. Ask them why the author chose this word. *Fissure means "a narrow opening or a crack," describing the shock the speaker feels.*

3. **READ AND CITE TEXT EVIDENCE** Remind students that figurative language includes similes, metaphors, personification, and imagery.

   Ⓒ **ASK STUDENTS** to describe the tone the figurative language creates in the poem. *Students should note that most of the figurative language involves inanimate objects coming to life. These images highlight the emptiness of life in Cuba. The "motes danced" and the light "darted" describe the stillness of Chicho's life.*

   Critical Vocabulary: motes (line 20) Have students share definitions of *motes*. Point out that the poet chose a short and accurate word rather than a phrase to maintain the rhythm of the line and poem.

   FOR ELL STUDENTS Explain that *clapboard* (line 8) is thin wood that is used to cover the side of a house.

25   as a man, *un hombre*, bend against the idea
          of leaving his country, call him loco.²
          What nobody counted on was that answers

          come on to those who sit in the
          quiet of their own countries, tranquil
30   in the **penumbra**, intent on hearing the song

          of a *tomegüín*³ as it calls for a mate
              to come nest in the shrubs out there,
          while in here, he witnesses how light

          fills the emptiness with the meaning of stay.

³ *loco*: crazy.
³ *tomegüín*: a small bird native to Cuba.

penumbra:
a place of partial light

4.   ◄ REREAD   Reread "The Stayer." How does the phrase "live in perpetual longing within exile" reflect the overall meaning of the poem?

Chicho chooses to stay in Cuba because he was born there and has history there. However, he lives in exile without his family and therefore is constantly "longing" for those who left.

SHORT RESPONSE

Cite Text Evidence   In what ways does each poet use figurative language to communicate a large or complex idea? **Cite evidence from the text.**

In "My Ceremony For Taking," the speaker uses figurative language to describe how bereft she feels after her parents' split. Using language such as "The way some carry their birth dirt for protection" and "My hair was my thanks," she communicates her longing for a ceremony to mend her broken self. In "The Stayer," the author uses figurative language to describe the light and sounds ("rain drummed like the gallop of spooked horses") and to evoke the sense of "longing within exile" that affects both the speaker and his uncle.

60

TO CHALLENGE STUDENTS . . .

Students have been interpreting figurative language in two poems. They will now create their own examples of figurative language.

ASK STUDENTS to work in pairs to write a couplet that includes original figurative language.

If necessary, you might get them started by having them write similes, comparisons, metaphors, or imagery to complete the following:

- as lonely as . . . *possibilities: the last dodo; a king; the moon*
- his heart felt like . . . *possibilities: lightning; a stone; porridge*
- my home is . . . *possibilities: everywhere; the Internet; empty*

DIG DEEPER

With the class, return to the Short Response. Have groups share their responses to the question.

ASK STUDENTS about the word choices the authors use in their poems.

- Why did the subject of "My Ceremony For Taking" need a ceremony? *She felt "fissured" and wanted to be whole.* Why did she leave her hair in the dirt? *She left part of herself in her old home and took some ancestral dirt in return.*
- Would the uncle in "The Stayer" have been happier if he had left Cuba? *No, he cannot bear the idea of leaving his homeland.* How does he keep himself content in his shack? *He wonders at the play of the light, the sounds of the rain, insects, and birds, and enjoys being at home.*

ASK STUDENTS to return to their Short Response answer and revise it based on the class discussion.

4.   **REREAD AND CITE TEXT EVIDENCE**

Ⓓ   **ASK STUDENTS** to explain in their own words the meaning of *exile* and *perpetual longing* in lines 17–18. Exile *is living away from one's own country.* Perpetual longing *is a yearning or desire that is continuous.*

Critical Vocabulary: penumbra (line 30) Have students share their definitions of *penumbra*—an area between light and shadow. You might want to point out that the word has a Latin root, meaning "almost shadow."

SHORT RESPONSE

Cite Text Evidence   Students' responses should include text evidence that supports their positions. They should:

- identify the central idea in each poem.
- cite examples of figurative language.
- explain how these examples support each central idea.

Sweet Sorrow

COLLECTION 4

Sweet Sorrow

"Love is the great intangible."

—Diane Ackerman

DRAMA

from The Tragedy of Romeo and Juliet
Prologue
Act II. Scene 2

William Shakespeare

from The Tragedy of Romeo and Juliet

Drama by William Shakespeare

 For more context and historical background, students can view the video "Biography: William Shakespeare" in their eBooks.

Why This Text

Students often have difficulty relating to Shakespeare's characters, who speak ornate sixteenth-century language, although people today experience many of the same emotions and longings. With the help of the close-reading questions, students will analyze the main characters and their motivations and desires. This close reading will lead students to an understanding of how characters' behavior and words can reveal their motivations.

Background Have students read the background about *Romeo and Juliet* and its author, William Shakespeare. They can also view the biography of Shakespeare in their eBooks. Tell students that Shakespeare is considered the finest playwright in the English language. Point out that many modern plays, stories, and even films are loosely based on his works.

AS YOU READ Remind students that a drama depends on dialogue to reveal characters' motivations. At what points in the play do Romeo and Juliet show what emotions move them to action?

 ### Common Core Support

- cite strong and thorough textual evidence
- analyze how complex characters develop over the course of a text and advance the plot
- analyze the impact of specific word choices on tone
- analyze an author's choices concerning how to structure a text and order events within it

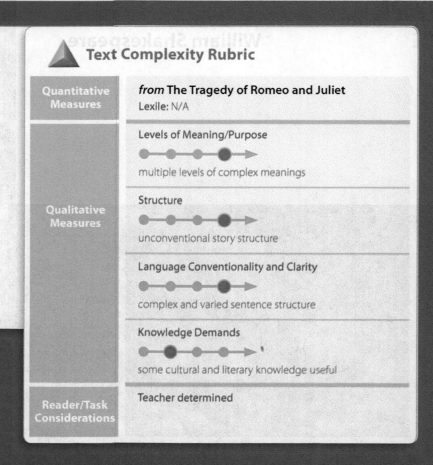

Text Complexity Rubric

Quantitative Measures

from **The Tragedy of Romeo and Juliet**
Lexile: N/A

Qualitative Measures

Levels of Meaning/Purpose
multiple levels of complex meanings

Structure
unconventional story structure

Language Conventionality and Clarity
complex and varied sentence structure

Knowledge Demands
some cultural and literary knowledge useful

Reader/Task Considerations
Teacher determined

Strategies for CLOSE READING

Analyze Character: Motivations

Students should read this excerpt from *Romeo and Juliet* carefully all the way through. Close-reading questions at the bottom of the page will help them understand how the characters' words reveal conflicting feelings and motivations. As they read, students should jot down comments or questions about the text in the margins.

WHEN STUDENTS STRUGGLE . . .

To help students analyze character's motivations, have them work in small groups to fill out a chart like the one shown below.

CITE TEXT EVIDENCE For practice in determining a character's motivations, ask students to give text examples and identify the speaker's motivation for each speech.

Character's Action or Words	Motivation
Romeo "By a name I know not how to tell thee who I am. My name, dear saint, is hateful to myself, Because it is an enemy to thee." (Act II, Scene 2, lines 53–56)	Romeo wants to be honest about his identity as a member of an enemy family, but he also wants to be someone who is pleasing to Juliet.
Juliet "If thou dost love, pronounce it faithfully. Or if thou thinkst I am too quickly won, I'll frown, and be perverse, and say thee nay." (Act II, Scene 2, lines 94–96)	Juliet wants Romeo to declare his love, but then she worries that he might think that she's throwing herself at him.

Background *It sounds like a love story ripped from the tabloids. Two teenagers fall in love. Then they learn that their parents hate one another. Murder and suffering follow, and by the end, a whole town is mourning. What love can—and cannot—overcome is at the core of* Romeo and Juliet, *considered by many to be the greatest love story of all time. This play by* **William Shakespeare** *(1564–1616) was one of his earlier works. It was probably first performed in the mid-1590s, when he would have been about thirty years old. As was the custom at that time, Shakespeare based his play on a story that already existed.*

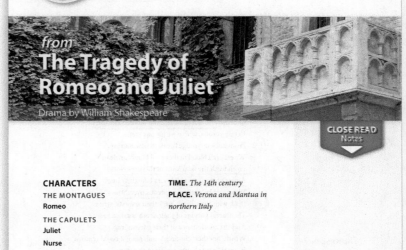

from
The Tragedy of Romeo and Juliet

Drama by William Shakespeare

CLOSE READ
Notes

CHARACTERS
THE MONTAGUES
Romeo

THE CAPULETS
Juliet
Nurse

OTHER
Chorus

TIME. *The 14th century*
PLACE. *Verona and Mantua in northern Italy*

63

1. **READ** ▶ As you read the Prologue, begin to cite text evidence.

- Circle text that describes the similar backgrounds of Romeo and Juliet.
- Underline clues that tell what will happen to the title characters.
- In the margin, explain how Shakespeare sets out one of the play's major themes—the conflict between love and hate.

The Chorus is an individual actor who serves as a narrator. He enters from the back of the stage to introduce and explain the theme of the play. His job is to "hook" the audience's interest by telling them just enough to quiet them down and make them eager for more. In this prologue, the Chorus explains the age-old feud between two prominent families of the Italian city of Verona.

PROLOGUE

[*Enter Chorus.*]

Chorus. Two households, both alike in dignity,
In fair Verona, where we lay our scene,
(A) From ancient grudge break to new **mutiny**,
Where civil blood makes civil hands unclean.
5   From forth the fatal loins of these two foes,
A pair of star-crossed[1] lovers take their life,[2]
Whose misadventured[3] piteous overthrows
(B) Doth with their death bury their parents' strife.
The fearful passage of their death-marked love,
10 And the continuance of their parents' rage,
Which, but their children's end, naught could remove,
Is now the two hours' traffic of our stage,
The which if you with patient ears attend,
What here shall miss, our toil shall strive to mend.
[*Exit.*]

mutiny:
rebellion

Shakespeare says that two people whose families have been feuding for years will fall in love.

[1] **star-crossed:** doomed. The position of the stars when the lovers were born was not favorable. In Shakespeare's day, people took astrology very seriously.
[2] **take their life:** are born, begin their lives.
[3] **misadventured:** unlucky.

2. **REREAD** Reread lines 6–10. What effect does the Chorus say that death will have on the remaining characters?

Death will end the feud between the families.

---

3. **READ** ▶ As you read lines 1–25 of Act II, Scene 2, continue to cite text evidence.

- Underline a metaphor that Romeo uses to describe Juliet.
- In the margin, explain Romeo's conflicting motivations (lines 13–14).

Prior to this scene, Romeo, a Montague, and his friends snuck into a masquerade ball given by the Capulet family. There, Romeo and Juliet, who is a Capulet, fall in love at first sight. Only after they talk and kiss do they discover they have fallen in love with the enemy. After the ball, Romeo hides in Lord Capulet's orchard, hoping for a chance to see Juliet on her balcony.

Act II

Scene 2 • Capulet's orchard.

[*Enter Romeo.*]

Romeo. He jests at scars that never felt a wound.[1]
[*Enter Juliet above at a window.*]
But soft! What light through yonder window breaks?
It is the East, and Juliet is the sun!
Arise, fair sun, and kill the envious moon,
5   Who is already sick and pale with grief
That thou her maid art far more fair than she.
Be not her maid, since she is envious;
Her vestal livery is but sick and green,
And none but fools do wear it; cast it off.
10 It is my lady; O, it is my love!
O that she knew she were!
She speaks, yet she says nothing. What of that?
(C) Her eye discourses; I will answer it.
I am too bold; 'tis not to me she speaks.
15 Two of the fairest stars in all the heaven,
Having some business, do entreat[2] her eyes
To twinkle in their spheres till they return.
What if her eyes were there, they in her head?
The brightness of her cheek would shame those stars

Romeo both wants to speak to Juliet and is afraid of speaking to her.

[1] **He jests at scars that never felt a wound:** Earlier, Romeo's friend Mercutio makes fun of love. Here, Romeo says he makes fun of it because he has never been wounded by it.
[2] **entreat:** beg, urge.

---

1. **READ AND CITE TEXT EVIDENCE**

   (A) ASK STUDENTS to cite evidence in lines 1–14 showing that the families have been feuding. *The families have an "ancient grudge" but also get into new quarrels ("mutiny"), and blood has probably been spilt in this feud ("Where civil blood makes civil hands unclean."). The parents feel "rage" that is ongoing.*

2. **REREAD AND CITE TEXT EVIDENCE**

   (B) ASK STUDENTS what other characters besides the two "star-crossed lovers" are mentioned in lines 6–10. What happens to them? *Students should identify the parents of the two lovers. The death of the lovers buries "their parents' strife." The parents' rage is ended only by the death of their children.*

   Critical Vocabulary: mutiny (line 3) Have students share their definitions of *mutiny*. Point out that in this context, *mutiny* also means "fighting."

3. **READ AND CITE TEXT EVIDENCE** Point out to students that Romeo's dialogue is in the form of a soliloquy—he is speaking aloud to himself (and of course to the audience). Juliet cannot hear him and indeed doesn't know he is there.

   (C) ASK STUDENTS to look at lines 10–14. How do these lines show that Romeo has two impulses that pull him in opposite directions? *Students may say that Romeo wishes that Juliet could know that he loves her. He wants to say something ("Her eye discourses; I will answer it.") but then feels that this would be too bold.*

   FOR ELL STUDENTS Point out that *art* (line 6), in this context, is not the noun, but an old form of *are*, of the verb *to be*.

D 20 As daylight doth a lamp; her eyes in heaven
Would through the airy region stream so bright
That birds would sing and think it were not night.
See how she leans her cheek upon her hand!
O that I were a glove upon that hand,
25 That I might touch that cheek!
Juliet. Ay me!
Romeo. She speaks.
O, speak again, bright angel! for thou art
As glorious to this night, being o'er my head,
As is a winged messenger of heaven
Unto the white-upturned wond'ring eyes
30 Of mortals that fall back to gaze on him
When he bestrides³ the lazy-pacing clouds
And sails upon the bosom of the air.

E **Juliet.** O Romeo, Romeo! Wherefore⁴ art thou Romeo?
Deny thy father and refuse thy name!
35 Or, if thou wilt not, be but sworn my love,
And I'll no longer be a Capulet.
Romeo [aside]. Shall I hear more, or shall I speak at this?
F **Juliet.** 'Tis but thy name that is my enemy.
Thou art thyself, though not⁵ a Montague.
40 What's Montague? It is nor hand, nor foot,
Nor arm, nor face, nor any other part
Belonging to a man. O, be some other name!
What's in a name? That which we call a rose
By any other name would smell as sweet.

---
³ **bestrides:** stands on.
⁴ **wherefore:** why.
⁵ **though not:** if you were not.

[Margin note:] Juliet wants Romeo to deny his father's name. If he will not, she promises to give up her name if he swears his love to her.

4. ◀ REREAD AND DISCUSS Reread lines 1–25 of Act II, Scene 2. In a small group, discuss how Romeo expresses his love for Juliet. To what does he compare her eyes?

5. READ ▶ As you read lines 26–53, continue to cite evidence.
• In the margin, explain what Juliet wants from Romeo (lines 33–36).
• Underline the first lines where one character knowingly addresses the other directly.
• Circle the lines where Juliet realizes she has been overheard.

---

45 So Romeo would, were he not Romeo called,
Retain that dear perfection which he owes⁶
Without that title. Romeo, doff⁷ thy name;
And for that name, which is no part of thee,
Take all myself.
Romeo. I take thee at thy word.
50 Call me but love, and I'll be new baptized;
Henceforth⁸ I never will be Romeo.
Juliet. What man art thou that, thus bescreened⁹ in night,
So stumblest on my counsel?¹⁰
Romeo. By a name
I know not how to tell thee who I am.
55 My name, dear saint, is hateful to myself,
Because it is an enemy to thee.
Had I it written, I would tear the word.
G **Juliet.** My ears have yet not drunk a hundred words
Of that tongue's utterance,¹¹ yet I know the sound.
60 Art thou not Romeo, and a Montague?
Romeo. Neither, fair saint, if either thee dislike.
H **Juliet.** How camest thou hither, tell me, and wherefore?
The orchard walls are high and hard to climb,
And the place death, considering who thou art,
65 If any of my kinsmen find thee here.

---
⁶ **owes:** owns, possesses.
⁷ **doff:** get rid of.
⁸ **henceforth:** from now on.
⁹ **bescreened:** hidden.
¹⁰ **counsel:** thoughts.
¹¹ **utterance:** speech.

6. ◀ REREAD Reread lines 38–49. What is Juliet saying about names here?

[Handwritten:] She thinks a name is unimportant. Just as a rose would still smell sweet if it weren't called a rose, so Juliet would still love Romeo if he weren't a Montague.

7. READ ▶ As you read lines 54–79, continue to cite textual evidence.
• Underline the text where Juliet worries about what will happen if her family finds Romeo on Capulet property.
• In the margin, explain what would distress Romeo more than facing death (lines 75–78).

---

4. REREAD AND DISCUSS USING TEXT EVIDENCE

D **ASK STUDENTS** what image Romeo uses to describe Juliet in lines 20–25. What does this image have in common with the other images that he has already used to describe her? *All of Romeo's images so far have to do with light: he says that "Juliet is the sun" (line 3); he compares her eyes to stars (lines 15–19), and in lines 20–25, he says that if her eyes were in the night sky, birds would think it was daylight.*

5. READ AND CITE TEXT EVIDENCE

E **ASK STUDENTS** what lines 33–36 reveal about Juliet's feelings for Romeo. *Students should understand that Juliet is declaring her love for Romeo even though she knows he is a Montague, her family's enemy.*

6. REREAD AND CITE TEXT EVIDENCE Nearly all the characters are allied with one side or another in the Capulet-Montague feud.

F **ASK STUDENTS** to reread lines 40–42 and then restate Juliet's lines in their own words. *Possible response: What does the name Montague mean? It's not a hand, foot, arm, face, or any physical thing that makes a man.*

7. READ AND CITE TEXT EVIDENCE

G **ASK STUDENTS** to look at lines 58–74. How do Juliet's statements about what the Capulets will do to Romeo reflect back to the Prologue? *They remind us that the Prologue has said that the conflict between the families is bloody and serious, and that a pair of lovers from the warring families will die.*

FOR ELL STUDENTS Challenge your ELL students to guess the meaning of *thee* ("you," object pronoun), *thy* ("your"), and *thou* ("you," subject pronoun).

Romeo. With love's light wings did I o'erperch these walls;
For stony limits cannot hold love out,
And what love can do, that dares love attempt.
Therefore thy kinsmen are no let[12] to me.
70 **Juliet.** If they do see thee, they will murder thee.
Romeo. Alack, there lies more peril in thine eye
Than twenty of their swords! Look thou but sweet,
And I am proof against their enmity.
Juliet. I would not for the world they saw thee here.
75 **Romeo.** I have night's cloak to hide me from their sight;
And but thou love me, let them find me here.
My life were better ended by their hate
Than death prorogued,[13] wanting of thy love.
Juliet. By whose direction found'st thou out this place?
80 **Romeo.** By love, that first did prompt me to enquire.
He lent me counsel, and I lent him eyes.
I am no pilot, yet, wert thou as far
As that vast shore washed with the farthest sea,
I would adventure for such merchandise.
85 **Juliet.** Thou knowest the mask of night is on my face;
Else would a maiden blush bepaint my cheek
For that which thou hast heard me speak tonight.

[12]**let:** hindrance, obstacle.
[13]**prorogued:** postponed.

Romeo says he'd rather die than not have Juliet's love.

8. ◀ REREAD Reread lines 62–79. Juliet has not spoken directly to Romeo of her feelings for him. What might be holding her back? What clues do you have about her emotions from her words here and earlier in Scene 2?

She has feelings for him because of the way she spoke before she knew he was listening, but now she seems mostly afraid that her relatives will come after him.

9. READ ▶ As you read lines 80–106, continue to cite textual evidence.

* In the margin, explain how Juliet feels about being overheard by Romeo (lines 85–89).
* Underline lines that show Juliet is worried that she will make a bad impression on Romeo by falling for him too easily.

68

> " *O gentle Romeo, if thou dost love, pronounce it faithfully.* "

Fain[14] would I dwell on form—fain, fain deny
What I have spoke; but farewell compliment!
90 Dost thou love me? I know thou wilt say "Ay";
And I will take thy word. Yet, if thou swear'st,
Thou mayst prove false. At lovers' perjuries,
They say Jove[15] laughs. O gentle Romeo,
If thou dost love, pronounce it faithfully.
95 Or if thou thinkst I am too quickly won,
I'll frown, and be perverse, and say thee nay,
So thou wilt woo; but else, not for the world.
In truth, fair Montague, I am too fond,
And therefore thou mayst think my 'havior light;
100 But trust me, gentleman, I'll prove more true
Than those that have more cunning to be strange.[16]
I should have been more strange, I must confess,
But that thou overheardst, ere I was ware,[17]
My true love's passion. Therefore pardon me,
105 And not impute this yielding to light love,
Which the dark night hath so discovered.

[14]**fain:** willingly.
[15]**Jove:** another name for the Roman god Jupiter, king of the gods.
[16]**strange:** aloof, cold.
[17]**ware:** aware.

Juliet is embarrassed that Romeo has overheard her. She'd like to deny what she said.

10. ◀ REREAD Reread lines 85–106. Explain the shifts in emotions Juliet experiences in this soliloquy.

At first Juliet is embarrassed, then she becomes frank, pleading, then shifting to anxiety, and doubt. She's afraid Romeo will lie about loving her, and then chides herself for loving him too quickly.

69

---

8. **REREAD AND CITE TEXT EVIDENCE** Point out that Juliet has already declared her longing for Romeo—but not directly to him, because she didn't know he was listening.

H **ASK STUDENTS** to look at lines 62–74 and compare what Juliet says to Romeo directly with what she said earlier. *Before, she spoke of him lovingly. Now, she doesn't speak of her love but worries that he will be killed if her family finds him there.*

9. **READ AND CITE TEXT EVIDENCE**

I **ASK STUDENTS** to read lines 85–89 and 93–99 and think about Juliet as if she were a real or fictional girl of today. How does she react when she realizes that she has been noticed by a boy she has feelings for? *She admits embarrassment by saying that she is blushing. She would love to take back what she said and worries that Romeo will think that she's too forward.*

10. **REREAD AND CITE TEXT EVIDENCE**

J **ASK STUDENTS** to read lines 90–106 and think about how Shakespeare treats the conflicting feelings of trust and doubt. What words does Juliet use to show that she wants to trust Romeo and to be trusted herself? *Juliet says "I will take thy word" (line 91), but then expresses doubt, "Thou mayst prove false" (line 92). She later asks Romeo to trust her, because she isn't like "those that have more cunning" (line 101).*

K **Romeo.** Lady, by yonder blessed moon I (swear,)
That tips with silver all these fruit-tree tops—
Juliet. O, (swear not by the moon) the inconstant moon,
110   That monthly changes in her circled orb,
Lest that thy love prove likewise variable.
Romeo. What shall I (swear) by?
Juliet.   Do not (swear) at all;
Or if thou wilt, (swear) by thy gracious self,
Which is the god of my idolatry,
115   And I'll believe thee.
Romeo.   If my heart's dear love—
Juliet. Well, do not (swear.) Although I joy in thee,
I have no joy of this contract[18] tonight.
It is too rash, too unadvised, too sudden;
Too like the lightning, which doth cease to be
120   Ere one can say "It lightens." Sweet, good night!
This bud of love, by summer's ripening breath,
May prove a beauteous flow'r when next we meet.
Good night, good night! As sweet repose and rest
Come to thy heart as that within my breast!
125   **Romeo.** O, wilt thou leave me so unsatisfied?
Juliet. What satisfaction canst thou have tonight?
Romeo. The exchange of thy love's faithful vow for mine.
Juliet. I gave thee mine before thou didst request it;
And yet I would it were to give again.
130   **Romeo.** Wouldst thou withdraw it? For what purpose, love?
Juliet. But to be frank and give it thee again.
And yet I wish but for the thing I have.
My bounty is as boundless as the sea,
My love as deep; the more I give to thee,
135   The more I have, for both are infinite.
L   I hear some noise within. Dear love, adieu!

<hr/>

[18] **contract:** declaration of love.

<hr/>

Juliet is uneasy about her relationship with Romeo. She's afraid everything is happening too quickly.

11. **READ** ▶ As you read lines 107–141, continue to cite textual evidence.

- Underline the line in which Romeo states what he wants of Juliet.
- Circle each time a character "swears" or promises something.
- In the margin, explain what Juliet is feeling.

[Nurse *calls within.*]
Anon[19], good nurse! Sweet Montague, be true.
Stay but a little, I will come again.
[*Exit.*]
Romeo. O blessed, blessed night! I am afeard,
140   Being in night, all this is but a dream,
Too flattering-sweet to be substantial.
N [*Re-enter* Juliet, *above.*]
M **Juliet.** Three words, dear Romeo, and good night indeed.
If that thy bent of love be honorable,
Thy purpose marriage, send me word tomorrow,
145   By one that I'll procure to come to thee,
Where and what time thou wilt perform the rite;
And all my fortunes at thy foot I'll lay
And follow thee my lord throughout the world.
Nurse [*within*]. Madam!
150   **Juliet.** I come, anon.—But if thou meanst not well,
I do beseech thee—
Nurse [*within*].   Madam!
Juliet.   By-and-by I come.
—To cease thy suit and leave me to my grief.
Tomorrow will I send.

<hr/>

[19] **anon:** right away.

Juliet and Romeo plan to get married tomorrow. Romeo will send a message to Juliet. The audience already knows that they will die.

12. **◀ REREAD** Reread lines 136–138. What happens in these lines? What other character is introduced here?

Juliet hears her nurse calling her and tells her she will be right there. She leaves and says she will come back to see Romeo one more time. The new character is Juliet's nurse.

13. **READ** ▶ As you read lines 142–169, continue to cite textual evidence.

- Underline the lines in which Juliet tells Romeo what she wants him to do.
- In the margin, explain the plans the couple makes. What does the audience already know from the prologue?

11. READ AND CITE TEXT EVIDENCE

K **ASK STUDENTS** to reread the exchange in lines 107–115, where Romeo is trying to make a vow of love to Juliet. Why does Juliet reject his first attempt to make this promise? *Romeo tries to swear by the moon, but Juliet worries that because the moon is so changeable in its appearance ("inconstant"), such a vow can't be trusted.*

FOR ELL STUDENTS Explain that the apostrophe in *flow'r* is used to shorten a noun—*flower*—so that it is one syllable. The apostrophe takes the place of the eliminated letter.

12. REREAD AND CITE TEXT EVIDENCE

L **ASK STUDENTS** how Shakespeare shows that another character is in the scene and identifies this character without having her appear. *The play doesn't show the nurse's response. She is identified only when Juliet addresses her as "good nurse."*

13. READ AND CITE TEXT EVIDENCE

M **ASK STUDENTS** to look back at the Prologue and review the words of the Chorus. Then ask them to reread lines 143–148. What do Romeo and Juliet look forward to in their future? What has Shakespeare said about their future? *They are beginning to speak of marriage. Juliet promises to "follow thee my lord throughout the world." However, the Chorus has said that they will die.*

Romeo.   So thrive my soul—
Juliet. A thousand times good night! [*Exit.*]
155   **Romeo.** A thousand times the worse, to want thy light!
Love goes toward love as schoolboys from their books;
But love from love, towards school with heavy looks.
[*Enter* Juliet *again, above.*]
Juliet. Hist![20] Romeo, hist! O for a falc'ner's voice[21]
To lure this tassel-gentle back again!
160   Bondage is hoarse and may not speak aloud;
Else would I tear the cave where Echo lies,
And make her airy tongue more hoarse than mine
With repetition of my Romeo's name.
Romeo!
165   **Romeo.** It is my soul that calls upon my name.
How silver-sweet sound lovers' tongues by night,
Like softest music to attending ears!
Juliet. Romeo!
Romeo.   My sweet?
Juliet.   What o'clock tomorrow
Shall I send to thee?
Romeo.   By the hour of nine.

[20]**hist:** listen.
[21]**a falc'ner's voice, to lure this tassel-gentle:** A falconer trains and cares for tame falcons
used for hunting; a tassel-gentle (or tiercel-gentle) is a variety of falcon.

---

14. ◀**REREAD** Reread lines 142–169. How does Shakespeare use Juliet's
leaving and returning to reveal more about Juliet's feelings?

Juliet keeps coming back to talk with Romeo. This shows that she is
in love with him. She can't bear to part with him, so she keeps
returning.

72

170   **Juliet.** I will not fail. 'Tis twenty years till then.
I have forgot why I did call thee back.
Romeo. Let me stand here till thou remember it.
Juliet. I shall forget, to have thee still stand there,
Rememb'ring how I love thy company.
175   **Romeo.** And I'll still stay, to have thee still forget,
Forgetting any other home but this.
Juliet. 'Tis almost morning. I would have thee gone—
And yet no farther than a wanton's[22] bird,
That lets it hop a little from her hand,
180   Like a poor prisoner in his twisted gyves,[23]
And with a silk thread plucks it back again,
So loving-jealous of his liberty.
Romeo. I would I were thy bird.
Juliet.   Sweet, so would I.
Yet I should kill thee with much cherishing.

[22]**wanton:** spoiled young girl.
[23]**twisted gyves:** shackles.

Juliet wants to
let him go
because it's
morning, but
also wants to
keep him by
her side.

---

15. **READ** ▶ As you read lines 170–190, continue to cite textual evidence.

- Underline the promises Romeo and Juliet make to each other.
- In the margin, explain in your own words the meaning of Juliet's words to
  Romeo (lines 177–182).

16. ◀**REREAD** Reread lines 177–186. Note some examples of
contradictions—saying opposite things—that Juliet says here. What
does this tell you about Juliet's motivations?

Juliet tells Romeo that she wants him to go because it's almost
morning, but she wants to keep him close. She says that she might kill
him with "much cherishing." She also refers to parting as "sweet
sorrow." These contradictions convey the idea that strong positive
and negative emotions can often be very close together.

73

---

14. REREAD AND CITE TEXT EVIDENCE   Remind students that
sometimes playwrights use stage directions as a tool to reveal
characters' motivations and actions.

Ⓝ **ASK STUDENTS** to reread the stage directions in these
lines. What is Juliet doing throughout this section? What kinds of
emotions would compel someone to keep coming back to
continue a conversation? *She keeps coming back out to talk with
Romeo. Students might suggest that she is overwhelmed and
confused by her emotions, so she wants to continue speaking.*

15. READ AND CITE TEXT EVIDENCE   The image in lines 177–182
may be challenging because of its archaic wording. Encourage
students to use footnotes as they read these lines.

Ⓞ **ASK STUDENTS** to read lines 177–182, along with the
footnotes. What are the figures in Juliet's image? *Encourage
students to visualize and identify a young girl holding a length of silk
cord attached to the leg of a tamed bird, the way a prisoner in leg
chains is tethered, so she can control its movement.*

16. REREAD AND CITE TEXT EVIDENCE

Ⓟ **ASK STUDENTS** to reread line 184. Explain that the word
should here means "would," not "ought to." What is the effect of
the contradiction in this line? *The destructive word* kill *and the
loving word* cherishing, *when combined, are jarring. They show
Juliet's heightened and confused emotions.*

185 Good night, good night! Parting is such sweet sorrow,
   That I shall say good night till it be morrow.
   [*Exit.*]
   Romeo. Sleep dwell upon thine eyes, peace in thy breast!
   Would I were sleep and peace, so sweet to rest!
   Hence will I to my ghostly father's[24] cell,
190   His help to crave and my dear hap[25] to tell.
   [*Exit.*]

   [24]**ghostly father:** priest, spiritual advisor.
   [25]**dear hap:** good fortune.

SHORT RESPONSE

Cite Text Evidence   Compare the tone of the Prologue to that of Act II, Scene 2. How might knowing the statements in the Prologue color an audience's view of the later scene between Romeo and Juliet? **Cite examples from the text** of the Prologue and Act II, Scene 2 as evidence.

The Prologue is tragic in tone. The chorus introduces the "ancient grudge" of the two families, and it announces that the love of the two main characters is doomed to end in death, using words such as "death," "blood," "rage," and "death-marked love" to create a feeling of disaster. The balcony scene is lyrical and hopeful in tone, as Romeo and Juliet declare their love for each other both in soliloquies and in dialogue. Shakespeare uses images of all kinds of light, including a comparison of Juliet to the sun and her eyes to stars. He also compares Juliet to an angel—a "winged messenger of heaven." Knowing that the love between Romeo and Juliet will end in their death gives the balcony scene an edge of tension. This tension is heightened by the dialogue from both characters about the difficulty of being from feuding families.

74

SHORT RESPONSE

Cite Text Evidence   Students' responses should include text evidence that supports their positions. They should:

- identify the tone of the Prologue, and give examples of wording that creates that tone.
- identify the tone of Act II, Scene 2, and give examples of wording that creates that tone.
- Explain the effect that the Prologue has on Act II, Scene 2.

TO CHALLENGE STUDENTS . . .

Shakespeare created many memorable heroines in addition to Juliet, and not all his heroines faced tragic endings. Some famous Shakespearean women who experienced happy endings include Viola in *Twelfth Night*, Portia in *The Merchant of Venice*, Titania in *A Midsummer Night's Dream*, and Rosalind in *As You Like It*.

ASK STUDENTS to research another Shakespearean heroine from his comedies. Students might make their choices from the ones mentioned above or choose other heroines. Have students read a synopsis of the comedy that stars the heroine they chose and then write a paragraph or two using their research, telling about their heroine's motivation. Have students compare their findings with those of other students.

DIG DEEPER

With the class, return to Question 10, Reread, on page 69. Have students share their responses.

ASK STUDENTS to cite the text evidence that led to their description of Juliet's shifting emotions.

- Have students identify Juliet's reaction that begins with line 85. What physical reaction does she describe to convey her feelings? *She is embarrassed. She says that she is blushing.*
- Ask what she says that she wishes she could do now that she knows that Romeo has heard her. *She would love to deny what she has said.*
- Ask what two conflicting feelings she displays in lines 90–99. *She says she'll trust Romeo if he says he loves her, but then she worries that he will prove false. Then she begs him to tell the truth. After that she worries that he will think she is too easily won and thinks she would have been more "strange" (aloof) if she had realized he could hear.*
- Have students explain what lines 100–106 show about her deepest feelings for Romeo. *She is honest about the fact that what she declared earlier were her true feelings ("my true love's passion") for Romeo.*
- Have students tell what effect they think such honesty ought to have on Romeo.

ASK STUDENTS to return to their answer and revise it based on the class discussion.

A Matter of Life or Death

COLLECTION 5

A Matter of Life or Death

"To endure what is unendurable is true endurance."

—Japanese proverb

from An Ordinary Man

Memoir by Paul Rusesabagina

Why This Text

Students do not always take the time to analyze how an author's rhetoric or style advances his or her point of view. *An Ordinary Man* is an account of one man's personal observations of a significant historical event: the 1994 genocidal slaughter in Rwanda. With the help of the close-reading questions, students will analyze Rusesabagina's rhetoric. This close reading will help students understand Rusesabagina's purpose for writing this memoir.

Background Have students read the background and the information about the author. Introduce the selection by telling students that the seeds for the 1994 violence in Rwanda were planted in 1916, when Belgian colonists devised a class system that divided the Tutsis and Hutus. In this class system, Tutsis were educated and Hutus were not. However, when Rwanda became free of Belgium in 1962, Hutus took power. From that point on, ethnic hatred between Tutsis and Hutus escalated.

AS YOU READ Ask students to pay attention to Rusesabagina's choices regarding content and word choice. How soon can they analyze his attitude toward the situation he describes?

 COMMON CORE

Common Core Support

- cite strong and thorough textual evidence
- determine the meaning of words and phrases as they are used in a text
- determine an author's purpose
- analyze how an author uses rhetoric to advance his or her purpose

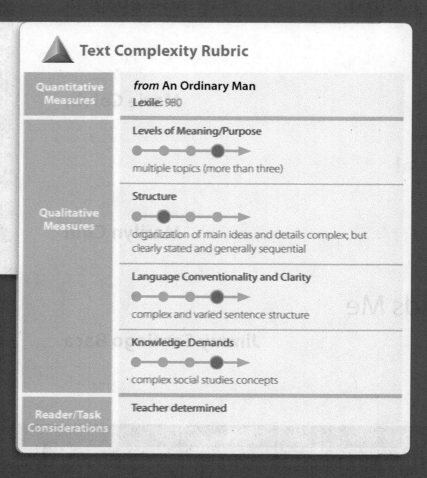

Text Complexity Rubric

Quantitative Measures	*from* An Ordinary Man
	Lexile: 980

Qualitative Measures

Levels of Meaning/Purpose

multiple topics (more than three)

Structure

organization of main ideas and details complex; but clearly stated and generally sequential

Language Conventionality and Clarity

complex and varied sentence structure

Knowledge Demands

complex social studies concepts

Reader/Task Considerations

Teacher determined

64

Strategies for CLOSE READING

Analyze Author's Purpose and Rhetoric

Students should read this text carefully all the way through. Close-reading questions at the bottom of the page will help them focus on a thorough analysis of the text. As they read, students should jot down comments or questions about the excerpt in the side margins.

WHEN STUDENTS STRUGGLE...

To help students analyze Rusesabagina's purpose, have them work in a small group to fill out a chart, such as the one shown below, as they analyze the text.

CITE TEXT EVIDENCE For practice analyzing an author's purpose, ask students to cite evidence of the author's rhetorical choices that advanced his purpose.

Title	"An Ordinary Man"
Language	"just how little I was able to accomplish" (line 65), "I am nothing more or less than a hotel manager" (lines 172–173), "Very simple: words" (line 129), "like a sports event" (lines 144–145)
Word Choice	"poisonous stream of rhetoric" (line 133), "avalanche of words" (line 146), "sea of fire" (line 175)
Tone	"hacked to death with machetes" (line 16), "butchered" (line 24), "looking at their own severed limbs" (line 58)
Parallel structure	"Rwanda was a failure . . . It started as a failure . . . It was the failure . . . It was a failure . . . It was a failure . . . It was the failure . . ." (lines 150–156), "Not the liquor, not money, not the UN." (line 162), "I was slippery . . . I acted friendly . . . I put cartons . . . I flattered them . . . I said whatever . . ." (lines 165–167)

Author's Purpose: to show that an "ordinary man" can make a difference through simple humanity

---

Background *In 1994, a mass genocide took place in the East African state of Rwanda when Hutus killed 800,000 men, women, and children over a period of 100 days. Although tensions existed between the Hutus and Tutsis (the two main ethnic groups in Rwanda) for hundreds of years, things came to a head on April 6, 1994, when a plane carrying the President of Rwanda, a Hutu, was shot down. Many perceived this as an attack by Tutsis, and the tensions between the two groups escalated into full-blown violence.* **Paul Rusesabagina** *lived through the genocide and wrote about the horrors in his memoir An Ordinary Man (from which this excerpt comes), which later became the film Hotel Rwanda.*

from An Ordinary Man

Memoir by Paul Rusesabagina

CLOSE READ
Notes

1. **READD ▶** As you read lines 1–43, begin to cite text evidence.

   • Underline the actions Rusesabagina took when the genocide broke out.
   • In the margin, explain what Rusesabagina has trouble understanding (lines 4–24).
   • Circle words and phrases that convey a tone of disgust and horror.

Ⓐ My name is Paul Rusesabagina. I am a hotel manager. In April 1994, when a wave of mass murder broke out in my country, I was able to hide 1,268 people inside the hotel where I worked.

When the militia and the Army came with orders to kill my guests, I took them into my office, treated them like friends, offered them beer and cognac, and then persuaded them to neglect their task that day. And when they came back, I poured more drinks and kept telling them they should leave in peace once again. It went on like this for seventy-six days. I was not particularly **eloquent** in these conversations. They were no different from

10 the words I would have used in saner times to order a shipment of pillowcases, for example, or tell the shuttle van driver to pick up a guest at the airport. I still don't understand why those men in the militias didn't just put a bullet in my head and execute every last person in the rooms upstairs but they didn't. None of the refugees in my hotel were killed. Nobody was beaten. Nobody was taken away and made to disappear. People were being hacked to death with machetes all over Rwanda, but that five-story building

eloquent:
well-spoken, moving

77

---

1. 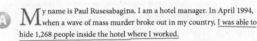 **READ AND CITE TEXT EVIDENCE**

Ⓐ ASK STUDENTS to use their underlined and circled text to explain what Paul Rusesabagina did in response to the violence that erupted in Rwanda in 1994. *Students should cite evidence that Rusesabagina saved people's lives by hiding them in a hotel (lines 2–3), negotiated with the militia to save lives (lines 5–8), and survived a genocide (lines 15–16).*

Critical Vocabulary: eloquent (line 9) Have students define *eloquent* as Rusesabagina uses it here. *Students should explain that Rusesabagina is humble in his explanation of his conversations with the militia. The words were "no different from the words I would have used in saner times to order a shipment of pillowcases, for example" (lines 9–11).*

prevailed:
triumphed

20 became a refuge for anyone who could make it to our doors. The hotel could offer only an illusion of safety, but for whatever reason, the illusion **prevailed** and I survived to tell the story, along with those I sheltered. There was nothing particularly heroic about it. My only pride in the matter is that I stayed at my post and continued to do my job as manager when all other aspects of decent life vanished. I kept the Hotel Mille Collines open, even as the nation descended into chaos and eight hundred thousand people were butchered by their friends, neighbors, and countrymen.

He has trouble
understanding
how he wasn't
killed along
with his hotel
guests. He
doesn't see
anything he
did as
"particularly
heroic."

B 30 It happened because of racial hatred. Most of the people hiding in my hotel were Tutsis, descendants of what had once been the ruling class of Rwanda. The people who wanted to kill them were mostly Hutus, who were traditionally farmers. The usual stereotype is that Tutsis are tall and thin with delicate noses, and Hutus are short and stocky with wider noses, but most people in Rwanda fit neither description. This divide is mostly artificial, a leftover from history, but people take it very seriously, and the two groups have been living uneasily alongside each other for more than five hundred years.

You might say the divide also lives inside me. I am the son of a Hutu farmer and his Tutsi wife. My family cared not the least bit about this when I was growing up, but since bloodlines are passed through the father in Rwanda, I am technically a Hutu. I married a Tutsi woman, whom I love with a fierce passion, and we had a child of mixed descent together. This type of blended family is typical in Rwanda, even with our long history of

40 racial prejudice. Very often we can't tell each other apart just by looking at one another. But the difference between Hutu and Tutsi means everything in Rwanda. In the late spring and early summer of 1994 it meant the difference between life and death.

2. ◀ REREAD Reread lines 25–43. How do Rusesabagina's words convey his feelings about the division between Hutus and Tutsis? What is his purpose in describing his family when explaining these differences? Support your answer with explicit textual evidence.

He thinks the divisions are artificial, as he himself is married to a
Tutsi whom he loves "with a fierce passion." He uses his family as an
example of a blended family—one comprised of both Tutsis and
Hutus—and explains that most Rwandan families are blended.

78

C Between April 6, when the plane of President Juvenal Habyarimana was shot down with a missile, and July 4, when the Tutsi rebel army captured the capital of Kigali, approximately eight hundred thousand Rwandans were slaughtered. This is a number that cannot be grasped with the rational

D 50 mind. It is like trying—all at once—to understand that the earth is surrounded by billions of balls of gas just like our sun across a vast blackness. You cannot understand the magnitude. Just try! Eight hundred thousand lives snuffed out in one hundred days. That's eight thousand lives a day. More than five lives per _minute_. Each one of those lives was like a little world in itself. Some person who laughed and cried and ate and thought and felt and hurt just like any other person, just like you and me. A mother's child, every one irreplaceable.

And the way they died . . . I can't bear to think about it for long. Many went slowly from slash wounds, watching their own blood gather in pools in the dirt, perhaps looking at their own severed limbs, oftentimes with the screams of their parents or their children or their husbands in their cars.

60 Their bodies were cast aside like garbage, left to rot in the sun, shoveled into mass graves with bulldozers when it was all over. It was not the largest genocide in the history of the world, but it was the fastest and most efficient.

At the end, the best you can say is that my hotel saved about four hours' worth of people. Take four hours away from one hundred days and you have an idea of just how little I was able to accomplish against the grand design.

The tone is of
shock and
disbelief.

sad; then
angry and
disgusted

despairing

3. READ ▶ As you read lines 44–73, continue to cite evidence.
• Underline words or phrases that convey Rusesabagina's tone.
• In the margin, describe the tone of each paragraph.
• Circle the resources Rusesabagina used to save the people hiding at the hotel.

4. ◀ REREAD Reread lines 44–55. What is Rusesabagina's purpose in these lines?

His purpose is to explain how the genocide happened and to impress
upon us the enormity of the horror involved and the sheer numbers
killed.

79

---

2. **REREAD AND CITE TEXT EVIDENCE**

B **ASK STUDENTS** to read their answer aloud to a partner. Then, have them read aloud the specific text that supports their answer. Finally, have them rewrite their response after receiving a peer review. _Students should explain that Rusesabagina uses his family as evidence (lines 37–39) and that the separation between Tutsis and Hutus is based on habit and stereotypes, not on reason or reality (lines 30–31)._

Critical Vocabulary: prevailed (line 19) Have students explain Rusesabagina's use of _prevailed_. What are the illusion and the reality, and which one prevailed? _Students should explain that the illusion of safety was the opposite of the reality of the genocide. Despite the odds, the illusion of safety prevailed. No one was killed in the hotel._

3. **READ AND CITE TEXT EVIDENCE**

C **ASK STUDENTS** to cite evidence for each description of Rusesabagina's tone. _"This is a number that cannnot be grasped with the rational mind" (lines 47–48); "I can't bear to think about it" (line 56); "how little I was able to accomplish" (line 65)._

4. **REREAD AND CITE TEXT EVIDENCE**

D **ASK STUDENTS** to add text evidence to their responses. _Students may cite evidence from lines 50–55 to show that Rusesabagina wants readers to understand the events and the enormity of the horror._

resigned

What did I have to work with? I had a five-story building. I had a cooler full of drinks. I had a small stack of cash in the safe. And I had a working telephone and I had my tongue. It wasn't much. Anybody with a gun or a machete could have taken these things away from me quite easily. My
70   disappearance—and that of my family—would have barely been noticed in the torrents of blood coursing through Rwanda in those months. Our bodies would have joined the thousands in the east-running rivers floating toward Lake Victoria, their skins turning white with water rot.

I wonder today what exactly it was that allowed me to stop the killing clock for four hours.

There were a few things in my favor, but they do not explain everything. I was a Hutu because my father was Hutu, and this gave me a certain amount of protection against immediate execution. But it was not only Tutsis who were slaughtered in the genocide; it was also the thousands of
80   moderate Hutus who were suspected of sympathizing with or even helping
(E) the Tutsi "cockroaches." I was certainly one of these cockroach-lovers. Under the standards of mad extremism at work then I was a prime
(F) candidate for a beheading.

"Image" is important because the hotel really wasn't safe or protected.

Another surface advantage: I had control of a luxury hotel, which was one of the few places during the genocide that had the image of being protected by soldiers. But the important word in that sentence is *image*. In the opening days of the slaughter, the United Nations had left four unarmed soldiers staying at the hotel as guests. This was a symbolic gesture. I was also able to bargain for the service of five Kigali policemen. But I
90   knew these men were like a wall of tissue paper standing between us and a flash flood.

Yet another of my advantages was a very strange one. I knew many of the architects of the genocide and had been friendly with them. It was, in a way, part of my job. I was the general manager of a hotel called the Diplomates, but I was eventually asked to take charge of a sister property, the nearby Hotel Mille Collines, where most of the events described in this book took place. The Mille Collines was *the* place in Kigali where the power

> I wonder today what exactly it was that allowed me to stop the killing clock for four hours.

classes of Rwanda came to meet Western businessmen and dignitaries. Before the killing started I had shared drinks with most of these men,
100   served them complimentary plates of lobster, lit their cigarettes. I knew the names of their wives and their children. I had stored up a large bank of favors. I cashed them all in—and then borrowed heavily—during the genocide. My preexisting friendship with General Augustin Bizimungu in particular helped save the Mille Collines from being raided many times over. But **alliances** always shift, particularly in the chaos of war, and I knew my supply of liquor and favors would run dry in some crucial quarters. Before the hundred days were over a squad of soldiers was dispatched to kill me. I survived only after a desperate half hour during which I called in even more favors.
110   All these things helped me during the genocide. But they don't explain everything.

Let me tell you what I think was the most important thing of all.

I will never forget walking out of my house the first day of the killings. There were people in the streets who I had known for seven years, neighbors of mine who had come over to our place for our regular Sunday cookouts. These people were wearing military uniforms that had been handed out by the militia. They were holding machetes and were trying to get inside the houses of those they knew to be Tutsi, those who had Tutsi relatives, or those who refused to go along with the murders.

alliance:
relationship; association

5. **READ ▶** As you read lines 74–109, continue to cite textual evidence.
   - Underline the advantages Rusesabagina had at the time of the genocide.
   - In the margin, explain why the word "image" is important in line 85.
   - Circle two instances in which Rusesabagina mentions being at risk.

6. **◀ REREAD AND DISCUSS** Reread lines 76–109. In a small group, discuss what else might have helped Rusesabagina survive the genocide.

7. **READ ▶** As you read lines 110–145, continue to cite textual evidence.
   - In the margin, explain why Rusesabagina included the story about Peter.
   - Underline text describing the "words" people had heard causing them to go "mad."

---

5. **READ AND CITE TEXT EVIDENCE**

(E) ASK STUDENTS to explain Rusesabagina's advantages and risks during the genocide. *Students should cite evidence from lines 81–83 to show that Rusesabagina was in danger. They should cite evidence from lines 84–86, 89, 92–93, and 101–102 to show Rusesabagina's advantages. Lines 107–109 are evidence of Rusesabagina's life being threatened.*

FOR ELL STUDENTS Encourage students to decipher the meaning of the noun *rot* (line 73). If they are having difficulty, help them by guiding them to the adjectival form, *rotten*.

6. **REREAD AND DISCUSS USING TEXT EVIDENCE**

(F) ASK STUDENTS to be prepared to share the results of their group discussions and to cite evidence to support their conclusions. *Rusesabagina describes his advantages as being on the "surface" in line 84. He credits his "large bank of favors" (lines 101–102) for saving his life and the lives of others in the hotel.*

7. **READ AND CITE TEXT EVIDENCE**

(G) ASK STUDENTS to cite text evidence to support their explanation of why Rusesabagina included the story about Peter. *Students should cite lines 121–122 as evidence that Peter was ordinary, lines 122–124 as evidence that Peter was gentle, and lines 125–126 as evidence that ordinary, gentle people had become murderers.*

Critical Vocabulary: alliance (line 105) Ask students to explain Rusesabagina's use of the word *alliance*.

Peter's story is an example of how seemingly normal people turned "mad" and violent.

120   There was one man in particular whom I will call Peter, though that is not his real name. He was a truck driver, about thirty years old, with a young wife. The best word I can use to describe him is an American word: *cool*. Peter was just a cool guy; so nice to children, very gentle, kind of a kidder, but never mean with his humor. I saw him that morning wearing a military uniform and holding a machete dripping in blood. Watching this happen in my own neighborhood was like looking up at a blue summer sky and seeing it suddenly turning to purple. The entire world had gone mad around me.

    What had caused this to happen? Very simple: words.

130   The parents of these people had been told over and over again that they were uglier and stupider than the Tutsis. They were told they would never be as physically attractive or as capable of running the affairs of the country. It was a poisonous stream of rhetoric designed to reinforce the power of the elite. When the Hutus came to power they spoke evil words of their own, fanning the old resentments, exciting the hysterical dark places in the heart.

    The words put out by radio station announcers were a major cause of the violence. There were explicit **exhortations** for ordinary citizens to break into the homes of their neighbors and kill them where they stood. Those 140 commands that weren't direct were phrased in code language that everybody understood: "Cut the tall trees. Clean your neighborhood. Do your duty." The names and addresses of targets were read over the air. If a person was able to run away his position and direction of travel were broadcast and the crowd followed the chase over the radio like a sports event.

exhortation:

urging by argument or appeal

8. ◀ REREAD   Reread lines 137–145. How does calling the hunt for Tutsis a "sports event" convey the tone of the narrative?

It conveys Rusesabagina's shock and disgust at his countrymen's behavior. To imagine people viewing the life or death battle of Tutsis as entertainment is horrifying. Small details like this make Rusesbagina's writing very compelling.

82

> " *Words . . . can also be powerful tools of life.* "

    The avalanche of words celebrating racial supremacy and encouraging people to do their duty created an alternate reality in Rwanda for those three months. It was an atmosphere where the insane was made to seem normal and disagreement with the mob was fatal.

150   Rwanda was a failure on so many levels. It started as a failure of the European colonists who exploited trivial differences for the sake of a divide-and-rule strategy. It was the failure of Africa to get beyond its ethnic divisions and form true coalition governments. It was a failure of Western democracies to step in and avert the catastrophe when abundant evidence was available. It was a failure of the United States for not calling a genocide by its right name. It was the failure of the United Nations to live up to its commitments as a peacemaking body.

    All of these come down to a failure of words. And this is what I want to tell you: Words are the most effective weapons of death in man's **arsenal.** 160 But they can also be powerful tools of life. They may be the only ones.

    Today I am convinced that the only thing that saved those 1,268 people in my hotel was words. Not the liquor, not money, not the UN. Just ordinary words directed against the darkness. They are so important. I used words in many ways during the genocide—to plead, intimidate, coax, cajole, and negotiate. I was slippery and evasive when I needed to be. I acted friendly toward despicable people. I put cartons of champagne into their car trunks. I flattered them shamelessly. I said whatever I thought it would take to keep the people in my hotel from being killed. I had no cause to advance, no ideology to promote beyond that one simple goal. Those words were my 170 connection to a saner world, to life as it ought to be lived.

    I am not a politician or a poet. I built my career on words that are plain and ordinary and concerned with everyday details. I am nothing more or

arsenal:

weapons

9. READ ▶   As you read lines 146–179, continue to cite textual evidence.
- Underline the reasons given for Rwanda's failure.
- Circle the biggest failure that led to the genocide.
- Underline the reasons Rusesabagina gives for his actions.

83

---

8. REREAD AND CITE TEXT EVIDENCE

H **ASK STUDENTS** to cite the specific text that supports their answer. *Students should cite evidence of the shock and disgust Rusesabagina felt at his countrymen's behavior and directions to kill their neighbors in lines 137–145.*

Critical Vocabulary: exhortation (line 138) Ask volunteers to explain why *exhortation* is a good choice here.

FOR ELL STUDENTS Clarify that the word *stream* (line 133) in this context is not a body of running water. In this text it means "a steady succession."

9. READ AND CITE TEXT EVIDENCE

I **ASK STUDENTS** to explain what Rusesabagina credits with the saving of the 1,268 people in his hotel. *He credits words.*

Critical Vocabulary: arsenal (line 159) Ask students to explain Rusesabagina's figurative use of *arsenal*. *Students should explain that Rusesabagina is using* arsenal *as a metaphor for the life-or-death power words can have.*

less than a hotel manager, trained to negotiate contracts and charged to give shelter to those who need it. My job did not change in the genocide, even though I was thrust into a sea of fire. I only spoke the words that seemed normal and sane to me. I did what I believed to be the ordinary things that an ordinary man would do. I said no to outrageous actions the way I thought that anybody would, and it still mystifies me that so many others could say yes.

10. **◀ REREAD** Reread lines 158–160. What does Rusesabagina mean when he says that words are powerful tools of life, that they "may be the only ones"?

He explains how he used words to convince the militias to leave the people in the hotel unharmed. He also explained how words had a part in causing the racial hatred and fanning the flames of the genocide. Words can save lives and also persuade others to kill.

SHORT RESPONSE

Cite Text Evidence   What is Rusesabagina's purpose in writing his book? What is the significance of the book's title, *An Ordinary Man*? Be sure to review your reading notes and **cite text evidence** in your response.

Rusesabagina wants people to know what happened in Rwanda, and what he did. He is humble, and reluctant to take credit for his deeds: "There was nothing particularly heroic about it." His language is plain but conveys the immensely horrific situation he lived through: "I can't bear to think about it for long . . . the best you can say is that my hotel saved about 'four hours' worth of people." The book's title echoes what Rusesabagina says. Readers know that his actions were extraordinary, but he doesn't think so. His only goal was to save as many lives as possible.

84

10. REREAD AND CITE TEXT EVIDENCE

J **ASK STUDENTS** to sum up Rusesabagina's belief about the power of words. *Students should cite evidence of his belief that only words saved the people in his hotel (lines 160–162), and strengthened his "connection to a saner world" (line 170).*

SHORT RESPONSE

Cite Text Evidence   Student responses will vary, but they should cite evidence from the article to support their analysis of Rusesabagina's purpose. Students should:

- determine Rusesabagina's purpose.
- explain the significance of the memoir's title.
- cite evidence from the text to support their explanation.

TO CHALLENGE STUDENTS . . .

For additional context on the historical origins of the Rwandan genocide, students can do research online.

ASK STUDENTS to cite evidence from "An Ordinary Man" and their online research to make a statement about the destructive power of stereotypes. What are the consequences of classifying a group of people as "a problem"?

DIG DEEPER

With the class, return to Question 4, Reread. Have students share their responses.

ASK STUDENTS to reread lines 44–55 to analyze how Rusesabagina uses rhetoric to support his purpose.

- What similes does Rusesabagina use to express his point? *"It is like trying—all at once—to understand that the earth is surrounded by billions of balls of gas just like our sun . . ." (lines 48–49). "Each one of those lives was like a little world in itself" (lines 52–53).* How do these examples support the author's purpose? *The first example demonstrates just how difficult it is to grasp the scale of the slaughter. The second example expresses that even a single death is a massive event.*

- How does Rusesabagina try to make the scale of the slaughter understandable to the reader? *He uses the total number of dead and the total amount of time, explaining first that it amounts to "eight thousand lives a day" (lines 51–52) and then to "more than five lives per minute" (line 52).* How does Rusesabagina's "math" support his purpose? *It allows the reader to grasp the enormity of the killing: more than 5 people a minute murdered continuously for one hundred days.*

ASK STUDENTS to return to the Short Response question and to revise it based on the class discussion.

Truth at All Costs

Speech by Marie Colvin

Why This Text

Students may have difficulty analyzing an argument without a thorough understanding of the writer's claims and evidence. Arguments such as this one, addressed in a speech by Marie Colvin, may use complex reasoning that becomes clear only with careful study. With the help of the close-reading questions, students will trace and evaluate Colvin's argument that being a war correspondent is worth the risk.

Background Have students read the background information about Marie Colvin, an American journalist who was killed in a Syrian attack while covering the siege of Homs for a British newspaper. Introduce the speech by pointing out that in her last television news broadcast, given on the day before she died, Colvin described the bombardment of Homs as the worst conflict she had ever encountered. Colvin believed that a war correspondent had to accept the risk to tell the truth about war, stating, "My job is to bear witness."

AS YOU READ Ask students to pay attention to the reasons Colvin gives to support her position that the job of a war correspondent is worth the risk. How soon into her speech can students begin to identify Colvin's point of view?

Common Core Support

- cite strong and thorough textual evidence to support text analysis
- analyze how the author unfolds a series of ideas and how they are developed
- delineate and evaluate an argument
- assess an author's claims and reasoning

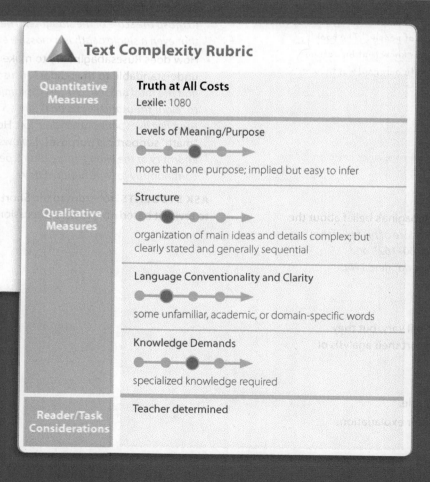

Text Complexity Rubric

Quantitative Measures	**Truth at All Costs** Lexile: 1080
Qualitative Measures	**Levels of Meaning/Purpose** more than one purpose; implied but easy to infer
	Structure organization of main ideas and details complex; but clearly stated and generally sequential
	Language Conventionality and Clarity some unfamiliar, academic, or domain-specific words
	Knowledge Demands specialized knowledge required
Reader/Task Considerations	Teacher determined

Delineate and Evaluate an Argument

Students should read this speech carefully all the way through. Close-reading questions at the bottom of the page will help them focus on a thorough analysis of the argument. As they read, students should record comments or questions about the text in the side margins.

WHEN STUDENTS STRUGGLE . . .

To help students analyze the reasons Colvin gives to support her claim that the job of a war correspondent is worth the risk, have students work in a small group to fill out a chart such as the one shown below as they analyze the speech.

CITE TEXT EVIDENCE For practice in tracing an argument, ask students to cite the evidence Colvin uses to support her claim.

CLAIM: *The job of a war correspondent is worth the risk.*

SUPPORT:

Reason 1: The war correspondent's mission is to give an accurate, unbiased report of the horrors of war—"to find the truth . . . in propaganda."

Reason 2: Combat journalists have great responsibilities to report on the horrors of war despite the huge risk to themselves and others.

Reason 3: War correspondents must report on humanitarian disasters and civilian atrocities to bring awareness to others.

Reason 4: War correspondents can make a difference in that they "speak the truth to power," and make the public aware of the dangers of war.

Reason 5: Although war reporting has changed technologically over the years, it still serves the same purpose—journalists need to bear witness to war.

Background *The award-winning journalist Marie Colvin (1956–2012) spent most of her professional life as the Middle East war correspondent for the British newspaper The Sunday Times. A fearless reporter, Colvin reported directly from war zones. In Tamil-Tiger-held Sri Lanka, she was hit by shrapnel and lost the use of her left eye. In 2012, while reporting on the shelling of civilians in Syria, Colvin and a French photojournalist were killed in a rocket attack. At her memorial, she was called "the bravest of the brave." She gave the following speech in 2010 to honor journalists who had died in war zones.*

Truth at All Costs

Speech by Marie Colvin

CLOSE READ
Notes

1. **READ ▷** As you read lines 1–20, begin to collect and cite evidence.
   - Underline text explaining the reason for Colvin's speech.
   - Circle lines describing what it means to cover a war.
   - in the margin, paraphrase the claim Colvin makes about the "mission" of war correspondents (lines 12–20).

Your Royal Highness, ladies and gentlemen, I am honoured and humbled to be speaking to you at this service tonight to remember the journalists and their support staff who gave their lives to report from the war zones of the 21st century. I have been a war correspondent for most of my professional life. It has always been a hard calling. But the need for frontline, objective reporting has never been more compelling.

Covering a war means going to places torn by chaos, destruction and death, and trying to bear witness. It means trying to find the truth in a sandstorm of **propaganda** when armies, tribes or terrorists clash. And yes,
10 it means taking risks, not just for yourself but often for the people who work closely with you.

propaganda:
biased
information

85

---

1. **READ AND CITE TEXT EVIDENCE**

A **ASK STUDENTS** to share their responses and then write one response that best states Colvin's claim in lines 12–20 about the basic "mission" of war correspondents. *Colvin believes the mission of a war correspondent is to report on the horrors of war accurately and without bias. They should cite lines 18–20 as evidence.*

Critical Vocabulary: propaganda (line 9) Have students share their definitions of *propaganda*. What does Colvin say is a war correspondent's role concerning propaganda? *She says that covering a war means trying to find the truth through all the biased information.*

FOR ELL STUDENTS Ask your ELL students to analyze the compound word *frontline* (line 6), identifying its two base words (*front* + *line*) and their meanings, and by defining the compound word. *It is the place where two armies face each other and fight during a war.*

The mission is to report accurately and objectively on war.

A B

bravado:
a showy display of courage

Despite all the videos you see from the Ministry of Defence or the Pentagon, and all the sanitised language describing smart bombs and pinpoint strikes, the scene on the ground has remained remarkably the same for hundreds of years. Craters. Burned houses. Mutilated bodies. Women weeping for children and husbands. Men for their wives, mothers children.

20 Our mission is to report these horrors of war with accuracy and without prejudice. We always have to ask ourselves whether the level of risk is worth the story. What is bravery, and what is **bravado**?

Journalists covering combat shoulder great responsibilities and face difficult choices. Sometimes they pay the ultimate price. Tonight we honour the 49 journalists and support staff who were killed bringing the news to our shores. We also remember journalists around the world who have been wounded, maimed or kidnapped and held hostage for months. It has never been more dangerous to be a war correspondent, because the journalist in the combat zone has become a prime target.

C I lost my eye in an ambush in the Sri Lankan civil war.[1] I had gone to
30 the northern Tamil area from which journalists were banned and found an unreported humanitarian disaster. As I was smuggled back across the internal border, a soldier launched a grenade at me and the shrapnel sliced into my face and chest. He knew what he was doing.

[1] **Sri Lankan civil war:** A 26-year civil war (1983–2009) between government troops and the Tamil Tigers, a minority separatist group, who fought to establish an independent state in Sri Lanka.

NATO forces guard the scene of a suicide bomb attack against British soldiers Wednesday, January 28, 2004, in the snow in Kabul, Afganistan.

Just last week, I had a coffee in Afghanistan with a photographer friend, Joao Silva. We talked about the terror one feels and must contain when patrolling on an embed[2] with the armed forces through fields and villages

D in Afghanistan . . . putting one foot in front of the other, steeling yourself each step for the blast. The expectation of that blast is the stuff of nightmares. Two days after our meeting, Joao stepped on a mine and lost both legs at the knee.

F 40 Many of you here must have asked yourselves, or be asking yourselves now, is it worth the cost in lives, heartbreak, loss? Can we really make a difference?

[2] **embed:** traveling with an army.

2. **REREAD** Reread lines 18–20. Explain the question that Colvin is asking. What idea is she emphasizing?

She is explaining that there is a difference between courage and boldness. She emphasizes the idea that part of the war reporter's job is to weigh the risks against the benefits of the story.

3. **READ** Read lines 21–39. Circle Colvin's claim about the danger war correspondents face today. Underline the evidence she cites to support her opinion.

86

4. **REREAD** Reread lines 33–39. How does the information Colvin gives in these lines support her argument about the danger of war reporting?

Colvin tells an anecdote about a conversation she had with a photographer about the difficulties of war reporting. She uses loaded language ("the stuff of nightmares") to support her point about the terror reporters feel, ending with the shocking news that this photographer has since lost both his legs.

5. **READ** As you read lines 40–52, continue to cite evidence.

- Circle the questions Colvin asks (lines 40–42).
- Underline the question raised by the newspaper.
- In the margin, explain the newspaper's point of view (lines 43–45).

87

---

2. **REREAD AND CITE TEXT EVIDENCE**

B **ASK STUDENTS** what distinction Colvin is making between bravery and bravado in lines 18–20. *Colvin is emphasizing that a war correspondent should weigh the level of risk against the benefits of getting a story to consider the difference between demonstrating real bravery and making a showy display of courage.*

3. **READ AND CITE TEXT EVIDENCE**

C **ASK STUDENTS** to determine how Colvin supports her opinion about the dangers faced by combat journalists today. *She relates the story of how she lost an eye in the Sri Lankan civil war (lines 28–32) and of how her photographer-friend Joao Silva stepped on a land mine and lost both his legs (lines 33–39).*

Critical Vocabulary: bravado (line 20) Have students compare their definitions of *bravado*, and ask for examples of people acting with bravado.

4. **REREAD AND CITE TEXT EVIDENCE**

D **ASK STUDENTS** to cite examples of Colvin's choice of words that support her argument. *The use of the word* steeling, *in "steeling yourself each step for the blast" (lines 36–37), creates the image of strength in the face of danger. The use of loaded language such as "the stuff of nightmares" (lines 37–38) appeals to her audience's emotions, and helps provide strong support for her argument.*

5. **READ AND CITE TEXT EVIDENCE**

E **ASK STUDENTS** to explain the newspaper's point of view concerning the risk Colvin took and the injury that resulted. *Students should cite evidence from lines 43–45 to explain that one newspaper suggested that Colvin took too great a risk in trying to get a story.*

The paper suggested that Colvin's injury was her own fault.

E I faced that question when I was injured. In fact one paper ran a headline saying, has Marie Colvin gone too far this time? My answer then, and now, was that it is worth it.

Today in this church are friends, colleagues and families who know exactly what I am talking about, and bear the cost of those experiences, as do their families and loved ones.

50 Today we must also remember how important it is that news organisations continue to invest in sending us out at great cost, both financial and emotional, to cover stories.

G We go to remote war zones to report what is happening. The public have a right to know what our government, and our armed forces, are doing in our name. Our mission is to speak the truth to power. We send home that first rough draft of history. We can and do make a difference in exposing the horrors of war and especially the atrocities that befall civilians.

The history of our profession is one to be proud of. The first war 60 correspondent in the modern era was William Howard Russell[3] of the Times, who was sent to cover the Crimean conflict[4] when a British-led coalition fought an invading Russian army.

Billy Russell, as the troops called him, created a firestorm of public indignation back home by revealing inadequate equipment, scandalous

repatriate:

to send back to one's country

treatment of the wounded, especially when they were **repatriated**—does this sound familiar?—and an incompetent high command that led to the folly of the Charge of the Light Brigade.[5] It was a breakthrough in war

[3] **William Howard Russell:** known as "Billy" Russell (1820–1907), Russell was a reporter who gained renown for his reporting on the Crimean War.

[4] **Crimean conflict:** a war (1853–1856) between the Russian Empire and an alliance of several European empires, including the British Empire; it was known as the first "modern" war.

[5] **Charge of the Light Brigade:** an ill-fated charge of British light cavalry against Russian forces during the Crimean War.

6. **REREAD AND DISCUSS** Reread lines 40–52. With a small group, discuss the questions Colvin asks and the answers she gives.

7. **READ** As you read lines 53–90, continue to cite text evidence.
- Underline what Colvin says the public have a right to know.
- Circle text that explains how war reporters make a difference (lines 53–57).
- Circle text that describes what Colvin calls "the real difficulty."

88

Our mission is to speak the truth to power.

reporting. Until then, wars were reported by junior officers who sent back dispatches to newspapers. Billy Russell went to war with an open mind, a 70 telescope, a notebook and a bottle of brandy. I first went to war with a typewriter, and learned to tap out a telex tape. It could take days to get from the front to a telephone or telex machine.

H War reporting has changed greatly in just the last few years. Now we go to war with a satellite phone, laptop, video camera and a flak jacket. I point my satellite phone to south southwest in Afghanistan, press a button and I have filed.

In an age of 24/7 rolling news, blogs and Twitters, we are on constant call wherever we are. But war reporting is still essentially the same— someone has to go there and see what is happening. You can't get that 80 information without going to places where people are being shot at, and others are shooting at you. The real difficulty is having enough faith in humanity to believe that enough people be they government, military or the man on the street, will care when your file reaches the printed page, the website or the TV screen.

8. **REREAD** Reread lines 73–79. Explain the contradiction Colvin introduces when she discusses how war reporting has changed.

When Colvin says war reporting has changed, she is talking primarily about changes in technology and protection. In other ways, war reporting hasn't changed because correspondents still need to go to dangerous places and see what's happening.

89

---

6. **REREAD AND DISCUSS USING TEXT EVIDENCE**

F **ASK STUDENTS** to cite evidence from the text about the questions Colvin asks and answers. *Students should cite evidence from lines 40–42, 43–45, and 50–52.*

7. **READ AND CITE TEXT EVIDENCE**

G **ASK STUDENTS** to explain how Colvin answers the question she asks in lines 53–57. How does it support the idea that a reporter is an eyewitness to history? *She says war journalists make a difference by telling people what is happening in a war (lines 53–55), by speaking "the truth to power" (line 55), and by exposing war atrocities (lines 56–58).*

Critical Vocabulary: repatriate (line 65) Have students explain *repatriate* and use it in a sentence.

8. **REREAD AND CITE TEXT EVIDENCE**

H **ASK STUDENTS** to cite evidence to support Colvin's contradictory claim in lines 73–79. *By citing the more sophisticated devices that journalists bring to the front today, such as a satellite phone, laptop, and video camera, which are far faster for filing a report than dispatches or telex machines, she is supporting her claim that war reporting has changed (lines 73–76). By recognizing that war journalists still have to go to the war-torn area to see what is happening (lines 78–79), she is supporting the contradictory claim.*

CLOSE READ
Notes

We do have that faith because we believe we do make a difference. And we could not make that difference—or begin to do our job—without the fixers, drivers and translators, who face the same risks and die in appalling numbers. Today we honour them as much as the front line journalists who have died in pursuit of the truth. They have kept the faith as
90   we who remain must continue to do.

9.   ◀ **REREAD**   Reread lines 81–90. What is Colvin's idea of faith? What does she say reporters need to believe in?

Colvin believes that war correspondents must have faith that their reporting makes a difference to someone who reads it.

SHORT RESPONSE

Cite Text Evidence   Explain whether or not Colvin convinced you that being a war correspondent is worth the risk. Review your reading notes, and evaluate the effectiveness of her argument. **Cite text evidence** in your response.

Possible response: Yes, it's worth the risk because war correspondents expose aspects of war that no other group does. They bear witness to the chaos and destruction of war and report on what their own governments and armies are doing in their name. Colvin cites the case of Billy Russell, who reported on the "inadequate equipment" and "scandalous treatment of the wounded" in the Crimean War, to bolster her case that the public needed to know this information. She also uses examples from her own life to show the dangers and the reasons behind the risk.

90

9.   **REREAD AND CITE TEXT EVIDENCE**

ⓘ **ASK STUDENTS** how Colvin's last paragraph adds power to her argument. *Colvin believes that correspondents must have faith in the idea that their war reporting will make a difference to people. Her last paragraph, in which she pays tribute to those who help war journalists do their job and who have died in the process, makes a strong emotional appeal to her audience about the need to take risks for the sake of telling the truth about the horrors of war.*

SHORT RESPONSE

Cite Text Evidence   Students should:

- explain whether or not they agree with Colvin's argument.
- give reasons for their point of view.
- cite specific evidence from the text to support their reasons.

TO CHALLENGE STUDENTS . . .

For more context about war reporters and photographers, students can conduct print or online research into other men and women who have followed these careers.

ASK STUDENTS to research other people who have reported on wars. Have each student pick one such person, conduct research, and present findings to the rest of the class.

- Point out that there have been people reporting from the battlefield for centuries. Students may find it rewarding to choose a person who lived during a period they themselves find interesting.
- Students should try to learn what got the person interested in reporting on wars. They should find out who the reporter or photographer worked for and what wars he or she covered.
- Encourage students to find out interesting details about the person they have picked. They might present quotes that offer insight into the person's world or photographs that show the person's work.

DIG DEEPER

With the class, return to Question 6, Reread and Discuss. Have students share the results of their discussion.

ASK STUDENTS whether they were satisfied with the outcome of their small-group discussions. Have each group share what their majority opinion was concerning the sufficiency of Colvin's evidence to support her conclusion—that being a war correspondent is worth the risk. What compelling evidence did the groups cite from the speech to support this opinion?

- Guide students to tell whether there was any convincing evidence cited by members holding the opposite opinion.
- Encourage groups to explain how they decided whether or not they had found sufficient evidence in the text to support their opinion. Did everyone in the group agree?
- After students have shared the results of their group's discussion, ask whether another group shared any findings they wish they had considered.

ASK STUDENTS to return to their Short Response answer and revise it based on the class discussion.

CLOSE READING NOTES

Poems About Survival

The Survivor

Poem by Marilyn Chin

Who Understands Me But Me

Poem by Jimmy Santiago Baca

Why These Texts

Readers of poetry may have trouble analyzing how poets use figurative language to create the poem's tone, or the poet's attitude toward the subject. With the help of the close-reading questions, students will identify words in the texts that create and convey the tone in each poem. They will also analyze how the tone can change within a poem.

Background Have students read the background information about survival and the biographical information about the two poets. Introduce the selection by telling students that the two poems they are about to read address the issue of survival. "The Survivor" explores how to survive in an unfriendly culture. "Who Understands Me But Me" explores the issue of surviving physical and mental imprisonment.

AS YOU READ Tell students to pay close attention to the figurative language in each poem and to think about the poet's attitude toward the subject.

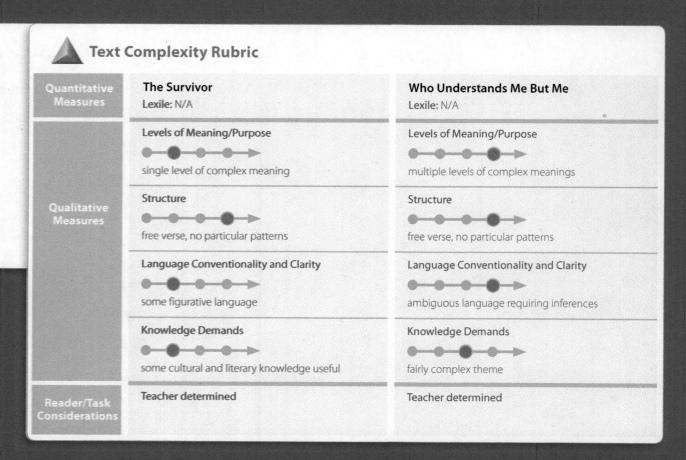

 Common Core Support

- cite strong and thorough textual evidence
- determine the meaning of words and phrases, including figurative and connotative meanings
- analyze the cumulative impact of specific word choices on meaning and tone

Text Complexity Rubric

	The Survivor Lexile: N/A	Who Understands Me But Me Lexile: N/A
Quantitative Measures		
Qualitative Measures	**Levels of Meaning/Purpose** single level of complex meaning	**Levels of Meaning/Purpose** multiple levels of complex meanings
	Structure free verse, no particular patterns	**Structure** free verse, no particular patterns
	Language Conventionality and Clarity some figurative language	**Language Conventionality and Clarity** ambiguous language requiring inferences
	Knowledge Demands some cultural and literary knowledge useful	**Knowledge Demands** fairly complex theme
Reader/Task Considerations	Teacher determined	Teacher determined

Strategies for CLOSE READING

Determine Figurative Meanings and Tone

Students should read each poem closely, noting the poet's word choices and thinking about the positive or negative connotations of those words. Close-reading questions will help students identify the words and images that create the tone of each poem. As they read, students should jot down in the margins notes or comments on each poem.

WHEN STUDENTS STRUGGLE . . .

To help students understand how figurative meanings create tone in a poem, have them work in small groups to fill out a chart like the one shown below.

CITE TEXT EVIDENCE For practice analyzing figurative meanings and the tone such language conveys, ask students to analyze this line from "The Survivor," identifying words that create tone.

Line from the Poem:
"All the tempests will render still; seas will calm, horses will retreat, voices to surrender."
Phrases with Figurative or Connotative Meanings That Convey the Tone:
"tempests will render still," "calm," "retreat," "surrender"
Description of the Tone:
The speaker is relieved that things will calm down.

Background *Someone once said, "It is not the strongest or the most intelligent who will survive but those who can best manage change." Adapting to new surroundings and learning how to survive in them is challenging, be it a new school, a new house, or even a new culture. In the selections below, poets* **Marilyn Chin** *and* **Jimmy Santiago Baca** *explore the theme of survival.*

Poems About
Survival

The Survivor . . . . Marilyn Chin
Who Understands Me But Me . . . . Jimmy Santiago Baca

Marilyn Chin *was born in Hong Kong and grew up in Portland, Oregon. Known as an "activist" poet, Chin frequently confronts themes of cultural assimilation and feminism. In an essay about American poetry, she writes, "My poetry both laments and celebrates my 'hyphenated' identity. . . My work is seeped with the themes and travails of exile, loss and assimilation. What is the loss of country if not the loss of self?"*

Jimmy Santiago Baca *has said, "I don't know if I would have lived had I not found poetry." He was born in New Mexico, of Apache and Chicano ancestry. Raised at first by a grandmother, he was a runaway at the age of 13. Convicted of drug charges, he was sentenced to a maximum security prison, where he began to turn his life around. He learned to read and write, and discovered his love of poetry. Since his release, he has published poetry, memoirs, and a screenplay.*

91

---

1. **READ** ▶ As you read lines 1–16 of "The Survivor," begin to collect and cite text evidence.

   • Circle repeating words in lines 1–4.
   • Underline text that describes the "you" in the poem.
   • In the margin, explain what must be relinquished in lines 15–16.

The Survivor
Marilyn Chin

B (Don't) tap your chopsticks against your bowl.
(Don't) throw your teacup against the wall in anger.
(Don't) suck on your long black braid and weep.
(Don't) tarry around the big red sign that says
5   "danger!"
   All the tempests will **render** still; seas will calm,
   horses will retreat, voices to surrender.
   That you have this way and not that,
   that your skin is yellow, not white, not black,
10   that you were born not a boychild but a girl,
   that this world will be forever puce-pink are just as well.
   Remember, the survivor is not the strongest or
   most clever;
   merely, the survivor is almost always the youngest.
A 15   And you shall have to relinquish that title
   before long.

render:
to cause to become

The title of "youngest" must be relinquished

2. **◀ REREAD** Reread lines 6–7 of "The Survivor." Determine how the tone of these lines differs from the preceding lines (1–5). Support your answer with explicit textual evidence.

In lines 6–7, the tone changes from one of rebellion and harshness to one of resolve and relief. Phrases such as "seas will calm, / horses will retreat" offer solace from the reprimands in the previous lines that begin with "Don't."

92

3. **READ** ▶ As you read lines 1–38 of "Who Understands Me But Me," begin to collect and cite text evidence.

   • Underline each thing the speaker lives without in lines 1–16.
   • In the margin, explain what setting the speaker evokes in lines 1–16.
   • In the margin, explain what the speaker finds when he follows the tracks (lines 30–38).

Who Understands Me But Me
Jimmy Santiago Baca

C They turn the water off, so I live without water,
they build walls higher, so I live without treetops,
they paint the windows black, so I live without sunshine.
they lock my cage, so I live without going anywhere,
5 they take each last tear I have, I live without tears.
they take my heart and rip it open, I live without heart.
they take my life and crush it, so I live without a future,
they say I am beastly and fiendish, so I have no friends.
they stop up each hope, so I have no passage out of hell,
10 they give me pain, so I live with pain,
they give me hate, so I live with my hate,
they have changed me, and I am not the same man,
they give me no shower, so I live with my smell,
they separate me from my brothers, so I live without brothers.
15 who understands me when I say this is beautiful?
who understands me when I say I have found other freedoms?

I cannot fly or make something appear in my hand,
I cannot make the heavens open or the earth tremble,
I can live with myself, and I am amazed at myself, my love,
20 my beauty,
I am taken by my failures, astounded by my fears,
I am stubborn and childish,
in the midst of this wreckage of life they **incurred**,
I practice being myself,
25 and I have found parts of myself never dreamed of by me,

These images of higher walls, black windows, and a locked cage evoke a prison setting.

incur:
become liable or subject to

93

---

1. **READ AND CITE TEXT EVIDENCE** Encourage students to use a dictionary to define any unfamiliar words such as *tarry* ("linger" or "hang around"), *puce* ("a dark red"), and *relinquish* ("give up").

   A ASK STUDENTS to identify what is meant by "that title" (line 15) that the speaker is told she will have to relinquish. *Being the youngest; presumably the speaker will soon no longer be the youngest.*

2. **REREAD AND CITE TEXT EVIDENCE**

   B ASK STUDENTS to describe the tone of lines 1–5 and to identify words that help create that tone. *The tone is one of anger and derision. The repetition of the word* Don't *and the phrase* in anger *help create the tone.*

   Critical Vocabulary: render (line 6) Have students share their definitions of *render*.

3. **READ AND CITE TEXT EVIDENCE** Have students think of a place that might have windows painted black, high walls, and locks on the doors. *jail, prison*

   C ASK STUDENTS to identify details in lines 1 through 4 that help them understand that people other than the speaker are controlling what he can and cannot do. *"they turn the water off," "they build walls higher," "they paint the windows black," "they lock my cage"*

   Critical Vocabulary: incur (line 23) Point out that *incur* can also mean "to bring down something upon oneself." Ask students to cite the details in line 23 that describe what "they" incurred. *"wreckage of life"*

   FOR ELL STUDENTS Tell students that a fiend is an evil or wicked person. Have students explain the meaning of *fiendish*.

goal:
to urge or prod

they were **goaded** out from under rocks in my heart
    when the walls were built higher,
    when the water was turned off and the windows painted black.
I followed these signs
30 like an old tracker and followed the tracks deep into myself,
    followed the blood-spotted path,
    deeper into dangerous regions, and found so many parts of myself,
    who taught me water is not everything,
    and gave me new eyes to see through walls,
35 and when they spoke, sunlight came out of their mouths,
    and I was laughing at me with them,
    we laughed like children and made pacts to always be loyal,
    who understands me when I say this is beautiful?

The speaker finds "so many parts of myself" and "new eyes to see through walls"

4. ◀ REREAD Reread lines 29–38 of "Who Understands Me But Me."
   Interpret the tone, and support your answer with textual evidence.

Baca's tone is triumphant. The inward journey, "I followed these signs like an old tracker and followed the tracks deep into myself," ends in triumph and joy as parts of the self are found: "sunlight came out of their mouths" and "we laughed like children."

SHORT RESPONSE

Cite Text Evidence   How do the two writers use figurative language to convey contrasting tones within their poems? **Cite textual evidence** in your response.

Both writers use powerful imagery to convey an experience of being confined by the expectations or actions of others. Chin's line, "Don't suck on your long black braid and weep," and Baca's line, "They turn the water off, so I live without water," are examples of this confinement. As Chin's poem finds resolve, "seas will calm," Baca's contrasting imagery is ecstatic: "new eyes to see through walls, and when they spoke, sunlight came out of their mouths." With the change of tone in each poem, we witness survival.

94

---

4. **REREAD AND CITE TEXT EVIDENCE**

Ⓓ **ASK STUDENTS** to find details in lines 29–38 that have figurative meanings that help them visualize the inward journey that the speaker made. *Possible responses: "deep into myself," "deeper into dangerous regions," "found so many parts of myself," "gave me new eyes to see through walls," "sunlight came out of their mouths," "I say this is beautiful."*

Critical Vocabulary: goad (line 26) Have students compare their definitions and use *goad* in a sentence. *For example: We had to goad her to write the essay.*

SHORT RESPONSE

Cite Text Evidence   Students' responses will vary, but they should cite evidence from the text to support their answers. Students should:

- describe the contrasting tones in each poem.
- explain how the tone of each poem changes.
- cite specific evidence from the text to support their ideas.

TO CHALLENGE STUDENTS . . .

The poems of Marilyn Chin and Jimmy Santiago Baca were written partly to explain how they managed to survive—and still manage to survive—under harsh circumstances. Everyone has difficulties to endure, and what might seem minor to one person can be a huge obstacle to another.

ASK STUDENTS to write a short poem about a person successfully struggling against adversity. The poem can be about themselves, someone they know, a fictitious character, or about a general situation. Encourage students to use language that suits the tone they want to communicate. Volunteers can share their completed poems with the rest of the class.

DIG DEEPER

With the class, return to Question 4, Reread. Have students share and discuss their answers.

ASK STUDENTS to work in small groups to describe the tone in the beginning of the poem. Have students cite evidence from the text to support their thinking.

- Have students identify the point at which the tone of defiance in the beginning of the poem begins to change. *(line 16)*
- Have students describe the tone of lines 16–25. *They may describe the tone as one of determination.*
- After students have traced the development of the tone throughout the poem, have volunteers from each group use their findings to read aloud for the class all or part of the poem "Who Understands Me But Me."

ASK STUDENTS to return to their response to Question 4, Reread, and expand it to include a discussion about how the tone changes as the poem progresses.

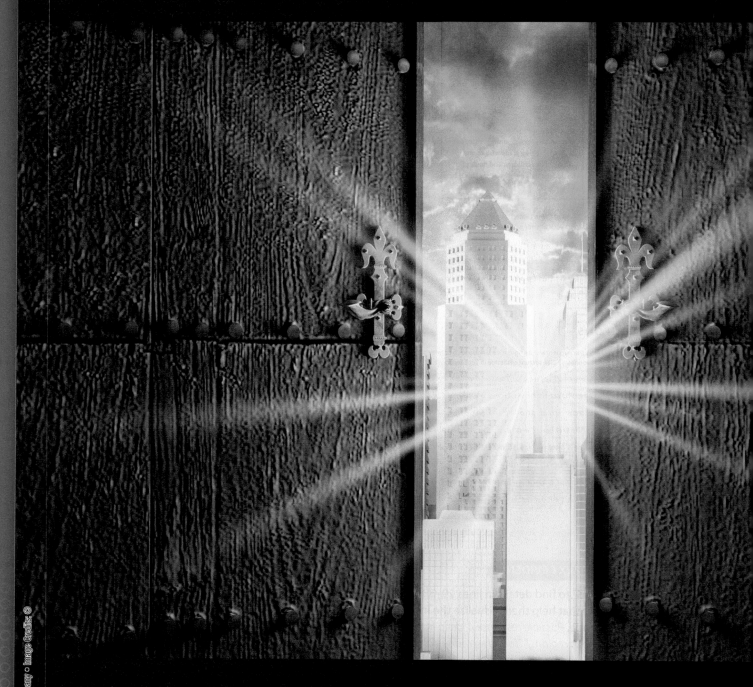

Heroes and Quests

Heroes and Quests

"If a journey doesn't have something to teach you about yourself, then what kind of journey is it?"

—Kira Salak

EPIC POEM

The Cyclops
from the Odyssey

Homer,
***translated by* Robert Fitzgerald**

NONFICTION

from The Good Soldiers

David Finkel

© Houghton Mifflin Harcourt Publishing Company ○ Image Credits: ©

For more context and historical background, students can view the video "Odysseus: Curse of the Sea" in their eBooks.

Why This Text

Students may have difficulty reading epic poetry. This excerpt from the *Odyssey* provides an opportunity to analyze how Odysseus faces conflict and interacts with other characters. With the help of close-reading questions, students will analyze the way Odysseus resolves a conflict when his men are trapped in a cave with a Cyclops. This close reading will lead students to analyze the character traits of an epic hero.

Background Have students read the background and the information about Homer. Introduce the selection by telling students that the speaker is Odysseus. He is going home after leading his army to victory in the Trojan War. For more background, students can view the video "Odysseus: Curse of the Sea" which provides background on the Trojan War and the start of Odysseus's journey.

AS YOU READ Ask students to note how Odysseus overcomes challenges. What will he learn when he faces the Cyclops?

Common Core Support

- cite strong and thorough textual evidence
- analyze how complex characters develop over the course of a text
- analyze how characters interact with other characters, advance the plot, and develop the theme
- determine the meaning of words and phrases as they are used in the text

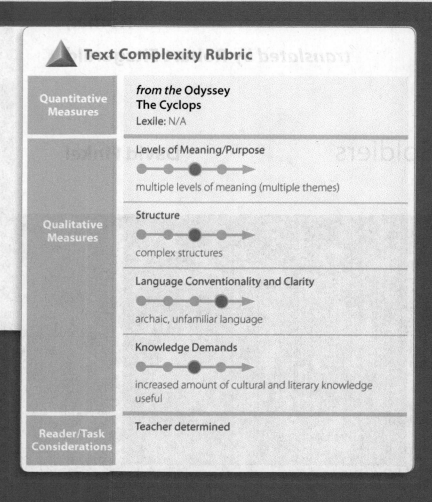

Text Complexity Rubric

Quantitative Measures	*from the* Odyssey **The Cyclops** Lexile: N/A
Qualitative Measures	**Levels of Meaning/Purpose** multiple levels of meaning (multiple themes)
	Structure complex structures
	Language Conventionality and Clarity archaic, unfamiliar language
	Knowledge Demands increased amount of cultural and literary knowledge useful
Reader/Task Considerations	Teacher determined

Strategies for CLOSE READING

Analyze Character: Epic Hero

Students should read this epic poetry carefully all the way through. Close-reading questions at the bottom of the page will help them focus on a thorough analysis of the text. As they read, students should jot down comments or questions about the poem in the side margins.

WHEN STUDENTS STRUGGLE . . .

To help students analyze Odysseus, have them work in a small group to fill out a chart, such as the one shown below, as they analyze the text.

CITE TEXT EVIDENCE For practice analyzing an epic hero, ask students to cite evidence of Odysseus's strengths and flaws.

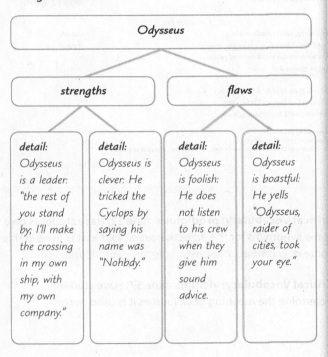

Odysseus			
strengths		**flaws**	
detail: Odysseus is a leader: "the rest of you stand by; I'll make the crossing in my own ship, with my own company."	detail: Odysseus is clever: He tricked the Cyclops by saying his name was "Nohbdy."	detail: Odysseus is foolish: He does not listen to his crew when they give him sound advice.	detail: Odysseus is boastful: He yells "Odysseus, raider of cities, took your eye."

Background No one knows for sure who **Homer** was, though the later Greeks believed he was a blind minstrel, or singer, who went from town to town. He is commonly credited with composing the Iliad (the story of the Trojan War) and the Odyssey. The Odyssey tells of the many adventures of a soldier named Odysseus on his ten-year journey home from the Trojan War. As this passage begins, Odysseus tells the story of encountering Polyphemus, the Cyclops.

from the Odyssey
The Cyclops

Epic Poem by Homer   Translated by Robert Fitzgerald

CLOSE READ
Notes

1. **READ ▶** As you read lines 1–20, begin to collect and cite text evidence.

- Underline text that reveals Odysseus's values.
- In the margin, summarize his description of the Cyclopes.
- Circle Odysseus's purpose for approaching the Cyclopes's island.

Ⓐ Ⓑ
"In the next land we found were Cyclops,[1]
giants, **louts**, without a law to bless them.
In ignorance leaving the fruitage of the earth in mystery
to the immortal gods, they neither plow
5   nor sow by hand, nor till the ground, though grain—
wild wheat and barley—grows untended, and
wine-grapes, in clusters, ripen in heaven's rain.
Cyclopes have no muster and no meeting,
no consultation or old tribal ways,
10   but each one dwells in his own mountain cave
dealing out rough justice to wife and child,
indifferent to what the others do. . . ."

[1] **Cyclopes:** refers to the creatures in plural; *Cyclops* is singular.

lout:
a stupid, rude person

The Cyclopes don't abide by laws, they don't farm, and they are brutes.

97

1. **READ AND CITE TEXT EVIDENCE** Explain to students that they can find Odysseus's values not only by looking at positive things he says about himself and his culture, but also by looking at negative things he says about the Cyclopes.

Ⓐ **ASK STUDENTS** to cite text that reveals Odysseus's values. *Students should cite evidence from lines 2, 4–5, and 8–9.* Ask them to use their circled text as evidence to draw a conclusion about Odysseus's character. Answers will vary. *They might say he is brave, or a leader.*

Critical Vocabulary: lout (line 2) How does this use of the word *lout* reveal Odysseus's values? *It is an insulting word, so readers can infer that Odysseus values the opposite of whatever is represented by the Cyclopes. For example, when Odysseus says the Cyclopes are "without a law to bless them" (line 2), readers can infer that Odysseus values law.*

Across the bay from the land of the Cyclopes was a lush, deserted island.
Odysseus and his crew landed on the island in a dense fog and spent days
feasting on wine and wild goats and observing the mainland, where the
Cyclopes lived. On the third day, Odysseus and his company of men set out
to learn if the Cyclopes were friends or foes.

"When the young Dawn with finger tips of rose
came in the east, I called my men together
15   and made a speech to them:

                'Old shipmates, friends,
the rest of you stand by; I'll make the crossing
in my own ship, with my own company,
and find out what the mainland natives are—
for they may be wild savages, and lawless,
20   or **hospitable** and god fearing men.'

hospitable:
generous

At this I went aboard, and gave the word
to cast off by the stern. My oarsmen followed,
filing in to their benches by the rowlocks,
and all in line dipped oars in the gray sea.

25   As we rowed on, and nearer to the mainland,
at one end of the bay, we saw a cavern
yawning above the water, screened with laurel,
and many rams and goats about the place
inside a sheepfold—made from slabs of stone

2. **REREAD** Reread lines 1–20. Based on the text, what inferences can you make about the values of Odysseus and his audience?

His criticism of the Cyclopes ("giants, louts, without a law to bless
them") shows that he values agriculture and community. He and his
audience also value friendship, hospitality, and respect for the gods.

3. **READ** As you read lines 21–60, continue to cite textual evidence.

- Underline text describing what Odysseus sees as he approaches land.
- Circle words Odysseus uses to describe the Cyclops.
- In the margin, explain what Odysseus brings with him to the island (lines 41–60).

30   earthfast[2] between tall trunks of pine and rugged
towering oak trees.

        A **prodigious** man

prodigious:
very big; huge

slept in this cave alone, and took his flocks
to graze afield—remote from all companions,
knowing none but savage ways, a brute
35   so huge, he seemed no man at all of those
who eat good wheaten bread; but he seemed rather
a shaggy mountain reared in solitude.
We beached there, and I told the crew
to stand by and keep watch over the ship;
40   as for myself I took my twelve best fighters
and went ahead. I had a goatskin full
of that sweet liquor that Euanthes'[3] son,
Maron, had given me. He kept Apollo's
holy grove at Ismarus; for kindness
45   we showed him there, and showed his wife and child,
he gave me seven shining golden talents[4]
perfectly formed, a solid silver winebowl,
and then this liquor—twelve two-handled jars
of brandy, pure and fiery. Not a slave
50   in Maron's household knew this drink; only
he, his wife and the storeroom mistress knew;
and they would put one cupful—ruby-colored,
honey-smooth—in twenty more of water,
but still the sweet scent hovered like a fume
55   over the winebowl. No man turned away
when cups of this came round.

He brings
liquor that was
given to him
as a gift and a
bag of food.

        A wineskin full

I brought along, and **victuals** in a bag,
for in my bones I knew some towering brute
would be upon us soon—all outward power,
60   a wild man, ignorant of civility.

victuals:
food

We climbed, then, briskly to the cave. But Cyclops
had gone afield, to pasture his fat sheep,
so we looked round at everything inside:

[2] **earthfast:** firmly grounded.
[3] **Euanthes:** a god in Greek mythology.
[4] **talents:** bars of gold or silver of a specified weight, used as money in ancient Greece.

---

2. **REREAD AND CITE TEXT EVIDENCE**

B **ASK STUDENTS** to cite evidence to support their inferences about the values of Odysseus and his audience. *Students may cite evidence that Odysseus values "law" (line 2), agriculture (lines 4–5), and community (lines 8–9). They may cite evidence that Odysseus values friendship (line 12) as well as hospitality and fear of god (line 20).*

3. **READ AND CITE TEXT EVIDENCE**

C **ASK STUDENTS** to cite text evidence to support their explanation of what Odysseus brings with him to the island. *Students should cite evidence that he took a "goatskin full of that sweet liquor" (lines 41–42) and "victuals in a bag" (line 57).*

Critical Vocabulary: hospitable (line 20) Have students explain how the word *hospitable* reveals a value of the ancient Greeks. *They considered hospitality a quality of refined people.*

Critical Vocabulary: prodigious (line 32) Have students give some synonyms for the adjective *prodigious* as it is used in this context. *enormous, huge, vast, colossal, gigantic, massive*

Critical Vocabulary: victuals (line 57) Have students determine the meaning of *victuals* as it is used here.

a drying rack that sagged with cheeses, pens
65 crowded with lambs and kids, each in its class:
firstlings apart from middlings, and the 'dewdrops,'
or newborn lambkins, penned apart from both.
And vessels full of whey[5] were brimming there—
bowls of earthenware and pails for milking.
70 My men came pressing round me, pleading:

(E)   'Why not
take these cheeses, get them stowed, come back,
throw open all the pens, and make a run for it?
We'll drive the kids and lambs aboard. We say
put out again on good salt water!'

                                              Ah,
75 how sound that was! Yet I refused. I wished
to see the caveman, what he had to offer—
no pretty sight, it turned out, for my friends.
We lit a fire, burnt an offering,
and took some cheese to eat; then sat in silence
80 around the embers, waiting. When he came
he had a load of dry boughs on his shoulder
to stoke his fire at suppertime. He dumped it
with a great crash into that hollow cave,
and we all scattered fast to the far wall.

---

[5] **whey:** the watery part of milk, which separates from the curds, or solid part, during the
making of cheese.

---

4. ◀ REREAD Reread lines 55–60. Why does Odysseus bring the liquor
   with him? Cite text evidence in your response.

He brings the liquor because he had a hunch that he might need to
incapacitate the Cyclops. The liquor was so good "No man turned
away when cups of this came round."

5. READ ▶ As you read lines 61–135, continue to cite textual evidence.

   • Underline text describing the "sound" request that Odysseus's men make.
   • Circle text that shows heroic qualities of Odysseus.
   • In the margin, explain the ancient Greek custom "to honor strangers"
     described in lines 115–120.

---

85 Then over the broad cavern floor he ushered
the ewes he meant to milk. He left his rams
and he-goats in the yard outside, and swung
high overhead a slab of solid rock
to close the cave. Two dozen four-wheeled wagons,
90 with heaving wagon teams, could not have stirred
the tonnage of that rock from where he wedged it
over the doorsill. Next he took his seat
and milked his bleating ewes. A practiced job
he made of it, giving each ewe her suckling;
95 thickened his milk, then, into curds and whey,
sieved out the curds to drip in withy baskets,[6]
and poured the whey to stand in bowls
cooling until he drank it for his supper.
When all these chores were done, he poked the fire,
100 heaping on brushwood. In the glare he saw us.

'Strangers,' he said, 'who are you? And where from?
What brings you here by sea ways—a fair traffic?[7]
Or are you wandering rogues, who cast your lives
like dice, and **ravage** other folk by sea?'

105 We felt a pressure on our hearts, in dread
of that deep rumble and that mighty man.
But all the same I spoke up in reply:

'We are from Troy, Achaeans, blown off course
by shifting gales on the Great South Sea;
110 homeward bound, but taking routes and ways
uncommon; so the will of Zeus would have it.
We served under Agamemnon,[8] son of Atreus—
the whole world knows what city
he laid waste, what armies he destroyed.
115 It was our luck to come here; here we stand,
beholden for your help, or any gifts
you give—as custom is to honor strangers.
We would entreat you, great Sir, have a care
for the gods' courtesy; Zeus will avenge
120 the unoffending guest.'

---

[6] **withy baskets:** baskets made from twigs.
[7] **fair traffic:** honest trade.
[8] **Agamemnon:** Commander of the Greek armed forces in the Trojan War.

ravage:
destroy
violently; ruin

It was a Greek
custom to
honor
strangers with
food and gifts.
Odysseus is
reminding the
Cyclops that
Zeus will
punish anyone
who mistreats
a guest.

---

4. REREAD AND CITE TEXT EVIDENCE

(D) **ASK STUDENTS** to cite the best piece of evidence to
support their explanation of why Odysseus brought the liquor.
Students should cite lines 58–59, "in my bones I knew some towering
brute would be upon us soon" to explain the need, and lines 55–56,
"No man turned away when cups of this came around" to show the
wine's effectiveness.

5. READ AND CITE TEXT EVIDENCE

(E) **ASK STUDENTS** to use their marked text as evidence to
describe Odysseus. _Students should point out that Odysseus refuses_
the sound advice he receives from his men (lines 71–75). They should
cite evidence of his heroism in his taking action despite his fear in
lines 105–107, his military service in lines 112–114, and his quick
thinking in lines 130–131.

Critical Vocabulary: ravage (line 104) Have students explain
how the word _ravage_ expresses the Cyclops's concern. _The word_
ravage implies violent destruction—the Cyclops is concerned that
Odysseus and his men may have come to loot.

He answered this
from his brute chest, unmoved:

'You are a ninny,
or else you come from the other end of nowhere,
F telling me, mind the gods! We Cyclopes
care not a whistle for your thundering Zeus
125   or all the gods in bliss; we have more force by far.
I would not let you go for fear of Zeus—
you or your friends—unless I had a whim to.
Tell me, where was it, now, you left your ship—
around the point, or down the shore, I wonder?'

130   He thought he'd find out, but I saw through this,
and answered with a ready lie:

'My ship?
Poseidon Lord, who sets the earth a-tremble,
broke it up on the rocks at your land's end.
A wind from seaward served him, drove us there.
135   We are survivors, these good men and I.'

Neither reply nor pity came from him,
but in one stride he clutched at my companions
and caught two in his hands like squirming puppies
to beat their brains out, spattering the floor.
140   Then he dismembered them and made his meal,
gaping and crunching like a mountain lion—
everything: innards, flesh, and marrow bones.
We cried aloud, lifting our hands to Zeus,
powerless, looking on at this, appalled;

6. ◀ REREAD AND DISCUSS Reread lines 122–127. With a small group,
discuss the Cyclops's response to Odysseus's reminder to be hospitable
and not anger Zeus. What does this response tell you about the
Cyclops's attitude toward the gods?

7. READ ▶ As you read lines 136–244, continue to cite text evidence.

• In the margin, explain Odysseus's reasoning in lines 148–154.
• Circle the epithet, or repeated descriptive phrase, in line 156. Explain the
meaning of these words in the margin.
• Underline text that outlines Odysseus's plan in lines 170–244.

145   but Cyclops went on filling up his belly
with manflesh and great gulps of whey,
then lay down like a mast among his sheep.
My heart beat high now at the chance of action,
and drawing the sharp sword from my hip I went
150   along his flank to stab him where the midriff
holds the liver. I had touched the spot
when suddén fear stayed me: if I killed him
we perished there as well, for we could never
move his **ponderous** doorway slab aside.
155   So we were left to groan and wait for morning.

When the young Dawn with fingertips of rose
lit up the world, the Cyclops built a fire
and milked his handsome ewes, all in due order,
putting the sucklings to the mothers. Then,
160   his chores being all dispatched, he caught
another brace of men to make his breakfast,
and whisked away his great door slab
to let his sheep go through—but he, behind,
reset the stone as one would cap a quiver.
165   There was a din of whistling as the Cyclops
rounded his flock to higher ground, then stillness.
And now I pondered how to hurt him worst,
if but Athena granted what I prayed for.
Here are the means I thought would serve my turn:

170   a club, or staff, lay there along the fold—
an olive tree, felled green and left to season
for Cyclops' hand. And it was like a mast
a lugger[9] of twenty oars, broad in the beam—
a deep-sea-going craft—might carry:
175   so long, so big around, it seemed. Now I
chopped out a six foot section of this pole
and set it down before my men, who scraped it;
and when they had it smooth, I hewed again
to make a stake with pointed end. I held this
180   in the fire's heart and turned it, toughening it,
then hid it, well back in the cavern, under
one of the dung piles in profusion there.

G

⁹ **lugger:** a small, wide sailing ship.

*If Odysseus
kills the
Cyclops, he
and his men
would be
trapped and
eventually die.*

ponderous:
*heavy and
massive*

*The reddish
rays of sunrise
brighten the
horizon.*

---

6. **REREAD AND DISCUSS USING TEXT EVIDENCE**

F **ASK STUDENTS** to cite evidence to support their inferences
in their discussion. Their evidence should be specific, and should
include line numbers. *Students should cite lines 123–124, "We
Cyclopes care not a whistle for your thundering Zeus."*

7. **READ AND CITE TEXT EVIDENCE**

G **ASK STUDENTS** to use their underlined text as evidence,
and explain Odysseus's plan. *Students should find evidence that
Odysseus crafted a weapon (lines 175–181), with which he planned
to blind the Cyclops (lines 184–186). He offered the Cyclops liquor
(lines 198–199), and got him drunk (lines 214–215). Then he said his
name was "Nohbdy" (line 219), and he used his weapon to blind the
Cyclops (lines 227–228, 233–237, and 241–242).*

Critical Vocabulary: ponderous (line 154) Discuss
denotations and connotations of *ponderous*. Remind students
that Homer wrote in Greek, and this is a translation. The
translator, Robert Fitzgerald, had to choose the best English
word to communicate Homer's description of the door.
Fitzgerald had to make choices that communicated Homer's
tone and poetry, not only his literal meaning. Why might
Fitzgerald have chosen this word? *The word* ponderous *has
several meanings: "having great weight," "awkward and unwieldy,"
"monotonous and tiresome." Each meaning can apply to the
doorway slab and the impression it makes on the men. The sound
of the word itself also adds to the feeling of the line.*

Now came the time to toss for it: who ventured
along with me? whose hand could bear to thrust
185 and grind that spike in Cyclops' eye, when mild
sleep had mastered him? As luck would have it,
the men I would have chosen won the toss—
four strong men, and I made five as captain.

At evening came the shepherd with his flock,
190 his woolly flock. The rams as well, this time,
entered the cave: by some sheep-herding whim—
or a god's bidding—none were left outside.
He hefted his great boulder into place
and sat him down to milk the bleating ewes
195 in proper order, put the lambs to suck,
and swiftly ran through all his evening chores.
Then he caught two more men and feasted on them.
My moment was at hand, and I went forward
holding an ivy bowl of my dark drink,
200 looking up, saying:

                    'Cyclops, try some wine.
Here's liquor to wash down your scraps of men.
Taste it, and see the kind of drink we carried
under our planks. I meant it for an offering
if you would help us home. But you are mad,
205 unbearable, a bloody monster! After this,
will any other traveller come to see you?'

He seized and drained the bowl, and it went down
so fiery and smooth he called for more:

'Give me another, thank you kindly. Tell me,
210 how are you called? I'll make a gift will please you.
Even Cyclopes know the wine-grapes grow
out of grassland and loam in heaven's rain,
but here's a bit of nectar and ambrosia!'[10]

 Three bowls I brought him, and he poured them down.
215 I saw the fuddle and flush[11] come over him,
then I sang out in cordial tones:

---

[10] ambrosia: food of the gods.
[11] fuddle and flush: the state of confusion and redness of the face caused by drinking
alcohol.

104

                              'Cyclops,
you ask my honorable name? Remember
the gift you promised me, and I shall tell you.
My name is Nohbdy: mother, father, and friends,
220 everyone calls me Nohbdy.'

                         And he said:
'Nohbdy's my meat, then, after I eat his friends.
Others come first. There's a noble gift, now.'

Even as he spoke, he reeled and tumbled backward,
his great head lolling to one side: and sleep
225 took him like any creature. Drunk, hiccupping,
he dribbled streams of liquor and bits of men.

Now, by the gods, I drove my big hand spike
deep in the embers, charring it again,
and cheered my men along with battle talk
230 to keep their courage up: no quitting now.
The pike of olive, green though it had been,
reddened and glowed as if about to catch.
I drew it from the coals and my four fellows
gave me a hand, lugging it near the Cyclops
235 as more than natural force nerved them; straight
forward they sprinted, lifted it, and rammed it
deep in his crater eye, and I leaned on it
turning it as a shipwright turns a drill
in planking, having men below to swing
240 the two-handled strap that spins it in the groove.
So with our brand we bored that great eye socket
while blood ran out around the red hot bar.
Eyelid and lash were seared; the pierced ball
hissed broiling, and the roots popped.

pike:
pointed stake

8. ◀ REREAD AND DISCUSS Reread lines 214–244. In a small group,
discuss why Odysseus tells the Cyclops his name is "Nohbdy" (line 219).
What is Odysseus planning?

9. READ ▶ As you read lines 245–339, continue to cite textual evidence.
   • In the margin, explain the action in lines 245–269.
   • Underline text that describes Odysseus's escape plan.
   • In the margin, explain how Odysseus and his men escape (lines 319–334).

105

FOR ELL STUDENTS Draw students' attention to the phrase *to toss
for it* (line 183). Then have them read the rest of the stanza and use the
context clues to infer the meaning: "to flip a coin to make a decision."

8. REREAD AND DISCUSS USING TEXT EVIDENCE

H ASK STUDENTS to cite text evidence to support their
predictions about what Odysseus is planning. Have small groups
discuss what has happened to the Cyclops, and what he is likely
to do next. How might the name Nohbdy be part of Odysseus's
plan? *Students may conclude that when the Cyclops says "Nohbdy,"
it will put the other Cyclopes off Odysseus's track.*

9. READ AND CITE TEXT EVIDENCE

I ASK STUDENTS to cite evidence to support their
explanation of the action in lines 245–269. *Students should cite
evidence that the Cyclops called for help (line 253), that he roars
"Nohbdy's tricked me" (line 262), and that the Cyclopes leave,
thinking there is nobody to fight (lines 264–268).*

Critical Vocabulary: pike (line 231) Ask students to explain the
meaning of *pike* as it is used here.

In a smithy¹²
245   one sees a white-hot axehead or an adze
       plunged and wrung in a cold tub, screeching steam—
       the way they make soft iron hale and hard—:
       just so that eyeball hissed around the spike.
       The Cyclops bellowed and the rock roared round him,
250   and we fell back in fear. Clawing his face
       he tugged the bloody spike out of his eye,
       threw it away, and his wild hands went groping;
       then he set up a howl for Cyclopes
       who lived in caves on windy peaks nearby.
255   Some heard him; and they came by divers¹³ ways
       to clump around outside and call:

                              'What ails you,
       Polyphemus? Why do you cry so sore
       in the starry night? You will not let us sleep.
       Sure no man's driving off your flock? No man
260   has tricked you, ruined you?'

                              Out of the cave
       the mammoth Polyphemus roared in answer:
       'Nohbdy, Nohbdy's tricked me, Nohbdy's ruined me!'
       To this rough shout they made a sage reply:
       'Ah well, if nobody has played you foul
265   there in your lonely bed, we are no use in pain
       given by great Zeus. Let it be your father,
       Poseidon Lord, to whom you pray.'

                              So saying
       they trailed away. And I was filled with laughter
       to see how like a charm the name deceived them.
270   Now Cyclops, wheezing as the pain came on him,
       fumbled to wrench away the great doorstone
       and squatted in the breach with arms thrown wide
       for any silly beast or man who bolted—
       hoping somehow I might be such a fool.
275   But I kept thinking how to win the game:
       death sat there huge; how could we slip away?

¹²**smithy:** blacksmith's shop.
¹³**divers:** diverse; various.

Polyphemus calls for the Cyclopes, but when they arrive, he explains that "Nohbdy" tricked him. Thinking there is nobody to fight, the Cyclopes leave.

106

I drew on all my wits, and ran through tactics,
       reasoning as a man will for dear life,
       until a trick came—and it pleased me well.
280   The Cyclops' rams were handsome, fat, with heavy
       fleeces, a dark violet.

                              Three abreast
       I tied them silently together, twining
       cords of willow from the ogre's bed;
       then slung a man under each middle one
285   to ride there safely, shielded left and right.
       So three sheep could convey each man. I took
       the woolliest ram, the choicest of the flock,
       and hung myself under his kinky belly,
       pulled up tight, with fingers twisted deep
290   in sheepskin ringlets for an iron grip.
       So, breathing hard, we waited until morning.

       When Dawn spread out her finger tips of rose
       the rams began to stir, moving for pasture,
       and peals of bleating echoed round the pens
295   where dams with udders full called for a milking.
       Blinded, and sick with pain from his head wound,
       the master stroked each ram, then let it pass,
       but my men riding on the pectoral fleece¹⁴
       the giant's blind hands blundering never found.
300   Last of them all my ram, the leader, came,
       weighted by wool and me with my **meditations.**
       The Cyclops patted him, and then he said:

       'Sweet cousin ram, why lag behind the rest
       in the night cave? You never linger so,
305   but graze before them all, and go afar
       to crop sweet grass, and take your stately way
       leading along the streams, until at evening

¹⁴**fleece:** wool covering a sheep's chest.

*meditations:
serious,
reflective
thought*

10. ◀ **REREAD AND DISCUSS** Reread lines 275–315. With a small group, discuss how Odysseus exemplifies an epic hero in these lines. Cite text evidence in your discussion.

107

FOR ELL STUDENTS Explain to students that the adjective *hale* (line 247) means "healthy."

---

10. (**REREAD AND DISCUSS USING TEXT EVIDENCE**

Ⓙ **ASK STUDENTS** to be prepared to share the results of their small-group discussions with the class. Students should be prepared to cite specific text evidence to support their analysis of Odysseus's heroism. *Students should cite Odysseus's use of his wits (line 277) to develop a plan to defeat his enemy.*

Critical Vocabulary: meditations (line 301) Have students determine the meaning of *meditations* as it is used here. What might the content of Odysseus's meditations have been? *Odysseus is probably thinking about whether or not his plan will work and if he and his men will escape from the Cyclops.*

Odysseus ties
his men under
the bellies of
the Cyclops's
sheep. The
blind Cyclops
cannot see the
men. In
addition, he
does not feel
them, because
the sheep are
tied together.

you run to be the first one in the fold.
Why, now, so far behind? Can you be grieving
310 over your Master's eye? That carrion rogue
and his accurst companions burnt it out
when he had conquered all my wits with wine.
Nohbdy will not get out alive, I swear.
Oh, had you brain and voice to tell
315 where he may be now, dodging all my fury!
Bashed by this hand and bashed on this rock wall
his brains would strew the floor, and I should have
rest from the outrage Nohbdy worked upon me.'

He sent us into the open, then. Close by,
320 I dropped and rolled clear of the ram's belly,
going this way and that to untie the men.
With many glances back, we rounded up
his fat, stiff-legged sheep to take aboard,
and drove them down to where the good ship lay.
325 We saw, as we came near, our fellows' faces
shining; then we saw them turn to grief
tallying those who had not fled from death.
I hushed them, jerking head and eyebrows up,
and in a low voice told them: 'Load this herd;
330 move fast, and put the ship's head toward the breakers.'
They all pitched in at loading, then embarked
and struck their oars into the sea. Far out,
as far off shore as shouted words would carry,
I sent a few back to the adversary:

335 'O Cyclops! Would you feast on my companions?
Puny, am I, in a Caveman's hands?
How do you like the beating that we gave you,
you damned cannibal? Eater of guests
under your roof! Zeus and the gods have paid you!'

11. **READ** ▶ As you read lines 340–404, continue to cite textual evidence.

- Underline text describing what Polyphemus does when he realizes Odysseus and his men have escaped and explain it in the margin (lines 340–352).
- Circle the protests made by Odysseus's crew.
- In the margin, paraphrase lines 366–375.

108

> ❝ **The blind thing in his doubled fury broke a hilltop in his hands and heaved it after us.** ❞

The Cyclops
throws the top
of a hill at
Odysseus's
ship. The wave
it creates
sends his ship
back to the
shore.

Ⓚ 340 The blind thing in his doubled fury broke
a hilltop in his hands and heaved it after us.
Ahead of our black prow it struck and sank
whelmed in a spuming geyser, a giant wave
that washed the ship stern foremost back to shore.
345 I got the longest boathook out and stood
fending us off, with furious nods to all
to put their backs into a racing stroke—
row, row, or perish. So the long oars bent
kicking the foam sternward, making head
350 until we drew away, and twice as far.
Now when I cupped my hands I heard the crew
in low voices protesting:

'Godsake, Captain!
Why bait the beast again? Let him alone!'
'That tidal wave he made on the first throw
355 all but beached us.'

'All but stove us in!'
'Give him our bearing with your trumpeting,
he'll get the range and lob a boulder.'

'Aye
He'll smash our timbers and our heads together!'
I would not heed them in my glorying spirit,
360 but let my anger flare and yelled:

'Cyclops,
if ever mortal man inquire

109

11. READ AND CITE TEXT EVIDENCE

Ⓚ **ASK STUDENTS** to cite their underlined and circled text as evidence, and explain one or more flaws in Odysseus's character. *Students should cite evidence from lines 340–344 to show that Odysseus's taunts resulted in great danger to himself and his crew. They should cite lines 352–361, and explain that Odysseus ignored good advice from his crew.*

WHEN STUDENTS STRUGGLE . . .

To help students understand Odysseus's character, have small groups work together to read aloud lines 335–397 as a script. Assign students to read the parts of Odysseus, the Cyclops, and the crewmen. Assign a narrator to read the lines that are not Odysseus's direct speech. Then, have students discuss what character strengths and character flaws Odysseus shows in these lines.

ASK STUDENTS to cite specific text evidence with line numbers to support their analysis of Odysseus's strengths and flaws. *Odysseus cannot control his temper—he endangers himself and his men when he taunts the Cyclops and calls out "How do you like the beating we gave you, you damned cannibal?" (lines 337–338) He is, however, a good leader: "I got the longest boathook out and stood fending us off" (lines 345–346) and encouraging his men to "row, row, or perish" (line 348).*

how you were put to shame and blinded, tell him
Odysseus, raider of cities, took your eye:
Laertes[15] son, whose home's on Ithaca!'

365   At this he gave a mighty sob and rumbled:

'Now comes the weird upon me, spoken of old.
A wizard, grand and wondrous, lived here—Telemus,[16]
a son of Eurymus; great length of days
370   he had in wizardry among the Cyclopes,
and these things he foretold for time to come:
my great eye lost, and at Odysseus' hands.
Always I had in mind some giant, armed
in giant force, would come against me here.
But this, but you—small, pitiful and twiggy—
375   you put me down with wine, you blinded me.
Come back, Odysseus, and I'll treat you well,
praying the god of earthquake to befriend you—
his son I am, for he by his avowal[17]
fathered me, and, if he will, he may
380   heal me of this black wound—he and no other
of all the happy gods or mortal men.'

Few words I shouted in reply to him:
'If I could take your life I would and take
your time away, and hurl you down to hell!
385   The god of earthquake could not heal you there!'

At this he stretched his hands out in his darkness
toward the sky of stars, and prayed Poseidon:
'O hear me, lord, blue girdler of the islands,
if I am thine indeed, and thou art father:
390   grant that Odysseus, raider of cities, never
see his home: Laertes' son, I mean,
who kept his hall on Ithaca. Should destiny
intend that he shall see his roof again
among his family in his father land,
395   far be that day, and dark the years between.'

[15]**Laertes:** King of Ithaca, an island in the Ionian Sea.
[16]**Telemus:** a prophet in Greek mythology.
[17]**avowal:** honest admission.

A prophet once told Polyphemus he would lose his eye, but he imagined "some giant" would take him down, not someone as small as Odysseus.

110

Let him lose all companions, and return
under strange sail to bitter days at home.'
In these words he prayed, and the god heard him.
Now he laid hands upon a bigger stone
400   and wheeled around, titanic for the cast,
to let it fly in the black-prowed vessel's track.
But it fell short, just aft the steering oar,
and whelming seas rose giant above the stone
to bear us onward toward the island.

             There

405   as we ran in we saw the squadron waiting,
the trim ships drawn up side by side, and all
our troubled friends who waited, looking seaward.
We beached her, grinding keel in the soft sand,
and waded in, ourselves, on the sandy beach.
410   Then we unloaded all the Cyclops' flock
to make division, share and share alike,
only my fighters voted that my ram,
the prize of all, should go to me. I slew him
by the sea side and burnt his long thighbones
415   to Zeus beyond the stormcloud, Cronus' son,
who rules the world. But Zeus disdained my offering:
destruction for my ships he had in store
and death for those who sailed them, my companions.

Now all day long until the sun went down
420   we made our feast on mutton and sweet wine,

Zeus's dissatisfaction signals further suffering for Odysseus. He will lose his ships and his companions.

---

12. **◀ REREAD** Reread lines 386–404. Explain Polyphemus's curse in your own words.

The Cyclops asks Poseidon to prevent Odysseus from returning home. If this cannot happen, he asks that the journey home take a long time, that Odysseus lose his crew, and that his home life be unhappy.

13. **READ ▶** Read lines 405–429. Underline text foreshadowing future events. In the margin, explain how the text "Zeus disdained my offering" furthers the plot (line 416).

111

FOR ELL STUDENTS The clause "Now comes the weird upon me" (line 366) may confuse students. Explain that the word *weird* means "very strange, or relating to the supernatural." Challenge students to analyze the clause and rewrite it in their own words. *Possible response: Now I am aware of something very strange.*

12. **REREAD AND CITE TEXT EVIDENCE**

Ⓛ ASK STUDENTS to cite text evidence to support their explanation of Polyphemus's curse. *Students should explain that the Cyclops asks Poseidon to prevent Odysseus from returning home (lines 390–391). If this cannot happen, he asks that the journey home take a long time (lines 392–395), that he lose his crew (line 396), and that his home life be unhappy: "bitter days at home" (line 397).*

13. **READ AND CITE TEXT EVIDENCE**

Ⓜ ASK STUDENTS how the foreshadowed future events— "destruction for my ships . . . death for those who sailed them . . ." (lines 417–418)—relate to the prayer the Cyclops made to Poseidon in the previous section. *The Cyclops pleaded that if Odysseus did manage to return to his home, "far be that day, and dark the years between" (line 395).*

till after sunset in the gathering dark
we went to sleep above the wash of ripples.

When the young Dawn with finger tips of rose
touched the world, I roused the men, gave orders
425   to man the ships, cast off the mooring lines;
and filing in to sit beside the rowlocks
oarsmen in line dipped oars in the gray sea.
So we moved out, sad in the vast offing,[8]
having our precious lives, but not our friends."

[8]**offing:** the part of the deep sea seen from the shore.

14.   ◀ **REREAD AND DISCUSS**   Reread lines 423–429. With a small group,
discuss why Odysseus and his men have mixed feelings as they leave
the land of the Cyclopes.

SHORT RESPONSE

Cite Text Evidence   In what ways is Odysseus an epic hero? Discuss his
strengths and his flaws. Review your reading notes, and **cite text evidence**
in your response.

Odysseus embodies Greek ideals: He is a military hero who "served
under Agamemnon"; he is of royal lineage—"Laertes' son"—and he
respects and remembers the gods. He has undertaken a long and
difficult journey and defeated a formidable opponent using his
intelligence: "I drew on all my wits, and ran through tactics,
reasoning as a man will for dear life, until a trick came." The
audience may identify with Odysseus's flaws: He is stubborn and
refuses to take other people's advice. He is also prone to taking rash
actions that endanger the lives of others.

112

---

14. ⬡ REREAD AND DISCUSS USING TEXT EVIDENCE

ASK STUDENTS to cite specific text evidence with line
numbers to support their explanation of why Odysseus and his
men have mixed feelings as they leave the land of the Cyclopes.
*Students should cite lines 428–429 as evidence that Odysseus and his
crew are happy to be alive, but sad about the friends that were killed
by the Cyclops.*

SHORT RESPONSE

Cite Text Evidence   Student responses will vary, but they should
cite evidence from the text to support their analysis of Odysseus as an
epic hero. Students should:

- analyze ways in which Odysseus's character fits the definition of an
  epic hero.
- provide a text-based analysis of Odysseus's character traits.
- cite strong textual evidence to support their response.

TO CHALLENGE STUDENTS . . .

For more context and interviews with historians about Odysseus
and his adventures, students can view the video "Odysseus: Curse
of the Sea" in their eBooks.

ASK STUDENTS to pay special attention to the interviews with
the various historians. What insights do they offer about Odysseus
and the customs of the ancient Greeks? *Students might say that the
historians emphasize Odysseus's curiosity (which is also attributed to
the Greek sense of adventure and exploration), the Greek tradition of
giving gifts to strangers, and the gruesomeness of the cannibalism of
the Cyclops.*

DIG DEEPER

With the class, return to Question 10, Reread and Discuss. Have
students share the results of their discussion.

ASK STUDENTS whether they were satisfied with the outcome
of their small-group discussions. Have each group share their
understanding of what made Odysseus a hero. What compelling
evidence did the groups cite from the text to support their
analysis?

- Ask students whether their understanding of what traits in
  Odysseus were heroic was unanimous, or whether group
  members had different ideas about what made Odysseus a
  hero.
- Ask students to talk about how their group worked together
  to identify text evidence. Was there agreement about which
  evidence was the strongest? Was there some evidence that
  was not included because it did not seem strong enough?
- Now that students have read the entire text, ask small groups
  to rejoin to locate additional evidence of Odysseus's heroic
  qualities. Does the additional evidence found in the text
  support the conclusions students made in their work on
  Question 10?

ASK STUDENTS to return to their Short Response answer and
revise it based on the class discussion.

from The Good Soldiers

Nonfiction by David Finkel

Why This Text

Students may finish reading a work of nonfiction without a complete understanding of the author's main points. Nonfiction selections such as this excerpt from the book *The Good Soldiers* by David Finkel may have more than one complex central idea. With the help of the close-reading questions, students will determine the central ideas by examining the specific details and other supporting evidence in the text.

Background Have students read the background and the information about the author David Finkel. Introduce the selection by telling students that Finkel is a Pulitzer Prize–winning journalist at the *Washington Post* and also a recipient of the MacArthur "genius grant" for his long-form narrative journalism. In awarding him the prize, the MacArthur Foundation singled out his book *The Good Soldiers*, published in 2009. Finkel compares getting a good news story to his camera's zoom lens. "I'm at wide angle," he says, "and I'm trying to get as close as possible and stay as long as I can."

AS YOU READ Ask students to pay close attention to the central ideas in this nonfiction selection and to the interactions among ideas or events in the text. How soon into the selection can students begin to identify a central idea?

Common Core Support

- cite multiple pieces of textual evidence
- determine a central idea and analyze its development over the course of the text, including how it is introduced, shaped, and refined by specific details
- analyze how the author unfolds a series of ideas or events
- explain how a series of ideas or events is developed in a text, and the connections that are drawn between them

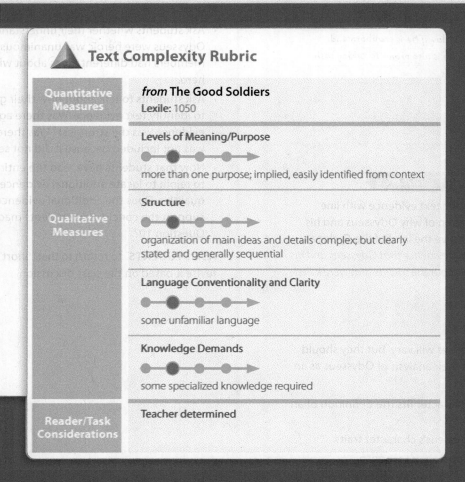

Text Complexity Rubric

Quantitative Measures

from **The Good Soldiers**
Lexile: 1050

Qualitative Measures

Levels of Meaning/Purpose

more than one purpose; implied, easily identified from context

Structure

organization of main ideas and details complex; but clearly stated and generally sequential

Language Conventionality and Clarity

some unfamiliar language

Knowledge Demands

some specialized knowledge required

Reader/Task Considerations

Teacher determined

Determine Central Idea and Cite Evidence

Students should read this text carefully all the way through. Close-reading questions at the bottom of the page will help them focus on a thorough analysis of the central idea of the selection and on how it is supported by specific details and evidence in the text. As they read, students should record comments or questions about the text in the side margins.

WHEN STUDENTS STRUGGLE . . .

To help students follow the selection's central idea, have them work in small groups to fill out a chart such as the one shown as they analyze this work of nonfiction.

CITE TEXT EVIDENCE For practice finding the central idea of an entire selection, ask students to examine how the central idea is developed over the course of the text, including how it emerges and is shaped and refined by specific details.

Central Idea	Supporting Details
Decency can be found even in war, and rules can be broken for the sake of doing what's right.	Line 35: Author's reflection, "How did moments of decency occur in this war?"
	Line 36: Cummings tells Izzy to bring his injured daughter to the base.
	Lines 60–65: Cummings decides to save Izzy's daughter, despite the rules.
	Lines 68–101: Cummings makes and receives phone calls to try to get Izzy's daughter treated at an American aid facility.
	Lines 117–122: Even though Cummings knows he has guessed wrong about which daughter is wounded, he has her taken into the American facility.
	Line 134: Author's reflection, "What do the rules say?"
	Lines 135–152: Neither Cummings nor anyone else cared what the rules said; all that mattered was saving the girl's life.

Background In 2007, President Bush announced a new strategy for the war in Iraq known as "the surge." Many Americans were skeptical about sending even more American forces overseas. Among the troops sent to Baghdad was the Second Battalion, 16th Infantry under the command of Lieutenant Colonel Ralph Kauzlarich. Reporter **David Finkel** embedded with this battalion for eight months, reporting from the front lines. His book, The Good Soldiers, tells the stories of the men from this battalion and the families they left behind.

from
The Good Soldiers

Nonfiction by David Finkel

CLOSE READ
Notes

1. **READ ▶** As you read lines 1–13, begin to collect and cite text evidence.

   • Circle the central idea in lines 1–13.
   • Underline details that support the central idea.
   • In the margin, make an inference about Kauzlarich's faith in Izzy.

If Kauzlarich were to pick a favorite among the Iraqis he had met, Qasim[1] would be up there, and so would Mr. Timimi, the civil manager, who day after day did whatever he did in his office with the big desk and the broken cuckoo clock.

But Izzy, his interpreter, was the one Kauzlarich had grown closest to and who had come to represent all the reasons Kauzlarich continued to find faith in the goodness of Iraqis, even after eleven deaths. Six years older than Kauzlarich, Izzy was a thin man with a melancholy face, the face of someone who understood life as something to be resigned to. At one point,
10 he had lived for a few years in New York City, as part of Iraq's delegation to the United Nations, which was when he became fluent in English. Now his job was to interpret everything said in Arabic to Kauzlarich, as well as what Kauzlarich wanted to say to Iraqis, no matter what it was.

Izzy signifies a "good" Iraqi compared to other Iraqis who may have killed Kauzlarich's men.

[1] **Kauzlarich, Qasim:** Lieutenant Colonel Ralph Kauzlarich, head of the 2-16 battalion. Colonel Qasim Ibrahim Alwan, head of a National Police battalion of Iraqis.

113

---

1. **READ AND CITE TEXT EVIDENCE**

A ASK STUDENTS to examine the details to identify the central idea in the first two paragraphs. *Students should cite text evidence in lines 5–7 to state the central idea—that of all the Iraqis Kauzlarich had met, Izzy, his interpreter, was the one he "had grown closest to," also citing lines 9–13 to show how the specific details about Izzy support the central idea.*

FOR ELL STUDENTS Some students may not understand *pick a favorite* in line 1. Ask a student who may know to explain what it means here. Then have students tell how the phrase suggests the central idea of lines 1–13. *Students should recognize that it sets up the central idea that of all the Iraqis he had met, Izzy was the one Kauzlarich liked best.*

> **He was standing on a street with his bleeding daughter at his side.**

Some Iraqis resented the Americans being there, and didn't like people who helped the Americans.

C
There were times when Iraqis would look at Izzy in obvious disgust, as if he were nothing more than a tool of the Americans. But he did his job enthusiastically, partly because of his affection for the United States—his older daughter, now seventeen, was born in New York City—and partly because of something that had happened over the summer when he had gone home to spend a few days with his family in central Baghdad.

20 Late one afternoon, a bomb had exploded just outside of his apartment building. Even by Baghdad standards it was a monstrous explosion. Twenty-five people died and more than one hundred others were injured, but seven miles away, no one on the FOB[2] knew anything about it until Brent Cummings's[3] cell phone rang and Izzy was on the other end, in a panic.

D
There had been an explosion, he said. His apartment was in ruins, his building was on fire, and one of his daughters had been badly injured by

[2] **FOB:** an abbreviation for Forward Operations Base, a base set up in special operations to support training or tactical operations.
[3] **Brent Cummings:** Major Brent Cummings, Kauzlarich's second in command.

2. **◄ REREAD** Reread lines 5–13. What is the author's purpose in explaining Kauzlarich's feelings about Izzy? Support your answer with explicit text evidence.

By stating that Izzy is the reason Kauzlarich still has "faith in the goodness of Iraqis," we can infer that Kauzlarich blames Iraqis for the "eleven deaths" of his men.

3. **READ ►** As your read lines 14–31, continue to cite text evidence.
   • Underline the text in lines 14–19 that hints at an important event.
   • In the margin, make an inference about some Iraqi attitudes toward Americans (lines14–19).
   • Circle the central idea that describes Izzy's situation in lines 25–31.

something that had pierced her head. He had taken her to a hospital, but there were so many other injured people that doctors had said there was nothing they could do, that she needed more help than they could give, and 30 so he was standing on a street with his bleeding daughter at his side, afraid that she was going to die.

"The only hope you have is to get her to an American hospital?" Cummings asked, repeating what Izzy had just said. Izzy started to answer. The cell phone went dead. "Izzy?" Cummings said. "Izzy?"

E How did moments of decency occur in this war?

"Izzy," Cummings said, calling him back. "Bring your daughter here." That was how.

"Oh thank you, sir. Thank you, sir," Izzy said.

F
And that's when things got complicated. Even this war had its rules, 40 and one of them covered who could be treated at an American aid facility. Americans could, of course, but Iraqis could not, unless they were injured by the American military, and only if the injury was life-threatening. Since the car bomb had been an Iraqi bomb, none of the injured was entitled to American care, including, it seemed, Izzy's daughter.

Cummings tells Izzy to bring his daughter to the base.

Even though terrible things happen in war, some acts of decency still occurred.

4. **◄ REREAD** Reread lines 20–31. How does the author develop the sense that events are unfolding quickly? Support your answer with explicit textual evidence.

By using reported dialogue, the author advances the action and adds immediacy. The blow-by-blow description of events—"his building was on fire" and "so he was standing on a street with his bleeding daughter at his side"—speeds up the pacing of the narrative.

5. **READ ►** As you read lines 32–49, continue to cite textual evidence.
   • In the margin, explain what Cummings tells Izzy to do.
   • Circle the author's reflections in lines 31–39.
   • In the margin, explain the reasoning behind the author's thoughts.

---

2. **REREAD AND CITE TEXT EVIDENCE**

B **ASK STUDENTS** to analyze the author's reason for explaining how Kauzlarich feels about Izzy. *Students should include specific references to lines 5–7 to explain the author's purpose. By admitting that Izzy is the reason Kauzlarich has retained his "faith in the goodness of Iraqis," students can infer that Kauzlarich blames the Iraqis for the death of eleven of his troops.*

3. **READ AND CITE TEXT EVIDENCE**

C **ASK STUDENTS** to work with a partner to write one response that infers what some Iraqis felt about the American troops. *Students should cite evidence from lines 14–19 to infer that some Iraqis felt contempt for the American troops and despised the Iraqis who helped the Americans.*

4. **REREAD AND CITE TEXT EVIDENCE**

D **ASK STUDENTS** to analyze how the author uses reported dialogue to convey the idea that events are unfolding at a rapid pace. *By having Cummings report what Izzy is saying on the phone (lines 25–31), students should recognize that the author is presenting a blow-by-blow description of the horrific events taking place and that the use of the run-on sentence in lines 27–31 adds a breathless pace to the narrative.*

5. **READ AND CITE TEXT EVIDENCE**

E **ASK STUDENTS** to work with a partner to write one response that explains the reasoning behind the author's rhetorical question to himself in line 35. *Students should cite evidence from lines 32–37 to explain that because Cummings tells Izzy to bring his daughter to the base for treatment, the author realizes that even in amid the horrors of war, some acts of decency can occur.*

It seems as if nobody knows what to do.

But Cummings had in mind Izzy's previous life, before he was an interpreter. If the daughter who was injured had been born in New York City, did that make her eligible? Could an American-born Iraqi who was injured by a non-American bomb receive medical care in an American military medical facility?

50 Cummings didn't know the answer. He phoned some doctors at the aid station, but they didn't know, either. He tried the FOB legal representative, but couldn't get through. He wasn't even sure which of the daughters had been injured—the one born in New York, or the eight-year-old who was born in Baghdad. He called Izzy back. The connection was terrible. He dialed again and again.

"Izzy . . . okay . . . where is your daughter that is from the United States?"

Again the phone went dead.

He called again. The connection kept breaking up. "Is your daughter
60 from the United States with you right now? . . . Is she hurt? . . . Which daughter is hurt? . . . Is she on the street with you? . . . You can't what? . . . What?"

Again the phone went dead, and at that point Cummings made a decision not to ask any more questions, just to assume what the answer would be. He was making a guess. He understood that. But with Kauzlarich

---

6. ◀ **REREAD** Reread lines 32–49. Explain Izzy's dilemma. Why does the author pose two questions in lines 45–49?

Izzy's daughter is badly injured and the Iraqi doctors said they couldn't help her. The author poses the questions to show the uncertainty of the situation. Even though Cummings has offered help, he does not know if he has the authority to do so.

---

7. **READ** ▶ As you read lines 50–67, continue to cite textual evidence.

- Circle each use of "didn't know" in lines 50–55. In the margin, explain how this repetition highlights the conflict.
- Underline the decision Cummings makes in lines 63–67. In the margin, draw an inference as to why he makes that decision.

---

away for a few hours on another FOB to attend a memorial ceremony, there was no one else to ask what to do.

He telephoned an officer in another battalion who controlled access to the FOB and whose approval would be needed for someone not in the
70 military to get through the gate without being turned away, detained, or shot. "Yes," he said. "I'm sure we can produce a birth certificate." He wondered whether such a certificate, if it even existed, had burned up in the fire. He checked the time. The sun was going down. A curfew would be in effect soon, at which point Izzy and his daughter wouldn't be allowed outside until sunrise. The officer kept asking questions. "We'll figure that piece out," Cummings said impatiently. "Right now, I just want to help the guy."

Next he called the battalion's physician and told him to be ready to treat one female, age unknown, in a matter of minutes. "A U.S. citizen," he
80 added, and then to that added, "maybe."

Next he tried Izzy again, to see how close he was to the FOB, and Izzy, his voice more panicked than before, said he wasn't close at all, that he was still on the street, still next to his daughter, trying to find a taxi. "Thank you, sir," he kept saying. "Thank you, sir. Thank you, sir."

There was nothing to do but wait. It wasn't as if a convoy could go pick up Izzy. He would have to get here on his own. The sun was almost down

He knows Izzy's daughter may die without help.

---

8. ◀ **REREAD** Reread lines 56–62. How do the short, choppy lines of dialogue affect the pacing of the narrative? Support your answer with explicit textual evidence.

They speed up the narrative adding urgency ("Is she hurt?"), and indicate Cummings's growing frustration (" You can't what? . . . What?").

---

9. **READ** ▶ As you read lines 68–129, continue to cite textual evidence.

- Underline every mention of a call made by or answered by Cummings.
- Circle statements Cummings makes that may not be true.
- Underline text explaining what Cummings knows when he sees Izzy and his family.

---

6. **REREAD AND CITE TEXT EVIDENCE**

F **ASK STUDENTS** what the author means when he says in line 39, "And that's when things got complicated." How do his two questions in lines 45–49 "flesh out" the complications of the situation? *Students should cite specific evidence in lines 39–44 to restate the complications and recognize that the two questions the author poses in lines 45–49 illustrate the uncertainty of the issue as to whether or not Izzy's daughter could be treated at an American medical facility.*

7. **READ AND CITE TEXT EVIDENCE**

G **ASK STUDENTS** what the central idea is in lines 63–67. Then have partners share their margin notes to infer why Cummings makes the decision he does. *Students should note that the central idea is that Cummings decides not to ask any more questions but "just to assume what the answers would be." They should infer from lines 63–67 that he feels that Izzy's daughter might die if he doesn't decide to have her treated at the base.*

8. **REREAD AND CITE TEXT EVIDENCE**

H **ASK STUDENTS** how the choppy dialogue in lines 56–62 and the use of ellipses affect the pace of the narrative. *Students should cite evidence in lines 56–62 to note that the short, choppy lines of dialogue and ellipses, which indicate that the cell phone connection is breaking up, indicate the urgency of the situation, while speeding up the action and the narrative pace.*

9. **READ AND CITE TEXT EVIDENCE**

I **ASK STUDENTS** to find and cite examples of each phone call made or received by Cummings in lines 68–101. How do the calls highlight the confusion of the situation while speeding up the narrative account? *Students should cite specific textual evidence in lines 68, 78, 81, 87, 89, 90, 95, 97, and 100 to indicate how the phone calls amplify the confusion since no one, including Cummings, has any answers, and how they highlight the immediacy and the frantic pace of the situation.*

now. A call came from an officer in another battalion who said he'd heard that the 2-16 had lost some soldiers somewhere. "No," Cummings said. Then another officer called saying he'd heard some soldiers had been

90 injured in an apartment bombing. Then another: the rumor was that some 2-16 soldiers had died in an EFP[4] attack.

"No, there are no injured Coalition Forces,"[5] Cummings kept saying. "It is an Iraqi—an Iraqi American—who was hurt. It is the interpreter's daughter."

He phoned Izzy again.

Still trying to find a taxi.

Another call, from the doctor: "I don't know the extent of the injuries . . . I don't know if he's even in a cab yet . . . I don't know if they're going to make it here before curfew."

100 Another call. It was Izzy. They were in a taxi. They were on the bridge, two minutes from the base.

Cummings hurried to the gate. It was dark now. The FOB's ambulance pulled up to receive the girl. Five minutes had gone by. Where was the taxi? Now the guards said they had stopped it in the distance and that there was no way it would be allowed any closer than it had gotten, which was somewhere out of sight. "Get a litter," Cummings yelled to the ambulance crew. Sprinting, he went out the gate, passing coils of razor wire and blast walls, and then stopping when he saw Izzy walking toward him, illuminated

110 by the headlights of the ambulance.

Izzy's clothing was filthy.

Next to him was his wife, who was crying.

On his other side was one of his daughters, the one born in New York, who appeared to be uninjured.

And in front of them all, wobbly but walking, was· a young girl with shiny purple sandals, blood all over her blue jeans, and a bandage covering the left side of her face.

It was the eight-year-old, the daughter born in Baghdad, the one who according to the rules had no standing whatsoever to be treated on the FOB.

120 "Izzy," Cummings called out, knowing right then that he had guessed wrong. He ran toward the family as other soldiers reached the girl. They lifted her up. She began crying. They carried her through the gate without stopping. They ran with her into the aid station, and as the doors swung

[4] **EFP:** Explosively Formed Penetrator, also known as Explosively Formed Projectile, a warhead designed to penetrate armor.
[5] **Coalition Forces:** military command led by the United States and its allies during the Iraq War.

118

> ". . . when he was unable to say anything else, he bowed his head, and then wiped his eyes . . ."

shut she cried out in Arabic for her father, who'd been told to remain in the lobby.

Izzy took a seat in a corner. Cummings stood nearby. "Was it a car bomb?" he asked after a while.

"No, sir," Izzy said. "It was two car bombs."

And then he said nothing more, not until one of the doctors came into the lobby to tell him that his daughter was going to be all right.

130 "Thank you, sir,' he managed to say, and when he was unable to say anything else, he bowed his head, and then wiped his eyes, and then followed the doctor into the treatment area, where he saw his Iraqi daughter surrounded by American doctors and medics.

What do the rules say?

At that moment, anyway, no one seemed concerned one way or another: not the doctors, not the family, and not Cummings, who stood at the very same spot he'd stood at as he watched Crow[6] die, watching once again.

The injuries to the girl were serious. There was a deep cut across her cheek, and worse, something had gone into the left side of her forehead,

140 near her temple, and was deeply embedded in bone. Izzy held her hand as the doctors wrapped her in a sheet, making sure to secure her arms tightly.

[6] **Crow:** Sergeant William Crow died from an EFP hit on his convoy in June 2007.

Sometimes it's okay to break the rules.

10. ◀ REREAD AND DISCUSS With a small group, discuss whether or not you think Cummings made the right decision.

11. READ ▶ As you read lines 130–152, continue to cite textual evidence.
- Circle the question the author asks.
- Underline text describing similarities between the Americans and the Iraqis.
- In the margin, explain a possible theme of lines 130–137.

119

WHEN STUDENTS STRUGGLE . . .

To help students understand how the central idea is shaped and refined by specific details, ask them to reread lines 117–120 and 134–136. Have small groups discuss the idea that Cummings's guess about the daughter had been wrong (the injured daughter was the one who had been born in Baghdad, not in New York), but that it was less important to him (and to the girl's family and doctors) than the idea that rules can be broken for the sake of doing the right thing— the central idea.

FOR ELL STUDENTS Point out that the word *litter* (line 106) is a multiple-meaning word and that in this context it means "a stretcher (or board) for carrying a sick or injured person." Ask students to give the other meanings of the word, such as "trash" or "offspring," and to use each meaning of the word in its own sentence.

10. REREAD AND DISCUSS USING TEXT EVIDENCE

J **ASK STUDENTS** to appoint a reporter for each group to cite specific textual evidence and line numbers to support their position about whether or not Cummings made the right decision to save Izzy's daughter in spite of the rules. *Students should cite lines 34–36, 39–44, 46–49, 63–67, 71, 79–80, 93, 117–20, 134–136, 138–141, 143–145, and 148–152.*

11. READ AND CITE TEXT EVIDENCE

K **ASK STUDENTS** to work with a partner or a small group to write the central idea in lines 130–137. What key point about life and people is the author communicating? *Students may cite specific textual evidence in lines 134–136 to state that the central idea is that sometimes it's okay to break the rules for the sake of doing what's right.*

The sound in Baghdad is of mourning; on the FOB the sound is joy and relief.

Her mother closed her eyes. The doctors leaned in. It took a while, and at the worst of it the little girl couldn't remain quiet, but then the doctors were showing her what they had pulled out—a thick piece of glass nearly two inches long.

The glass had been part of an apartment that no longer existed, in a section of Baghdad where the sounds that night were of mourning.

But here on the FOB, the sounds were of a mother whose home was ruined kissing her daughter's face, and a father whose home was ruined 150 kissing his daughter's hand, and a little girl whose home was ruined saying something in Arabic that caused her family to smile, and Cummings saying quietly in English, "Man, I haven't felt this good since I got to this hellhole."

---

12. **◄ REREAD** Reread lines 146–152. In the margin, compare the sounds described in these lines. What mood does each create?

SHORT RESPONSE

Cite Text Evidence What is the central idea of this piece? Explain how the author introduces and develops that idea over the course of the text. Review your reading notes and **cite text evidence**.

The central idea of this selection is that decency can be found even during war, and rules can be broken for the sake of doing what is right. The idea is introduced by the author's reflection, a rhetorical question: "How did moments of decency occur in this war?" The response is in Cummings's decision to save Izzy's daughter's life, despites the rules. The central idea is shaped and refined by description and dialogue. It is reiterated by the author at the end of the text, when he asks, "What do the rules say?" He responds by saying that no one is concerned with the rules in the face of the larger fact that a girl's life has been saved.

120

---

12. REREAD AND CITE TEXT EVIDENCE

ASK STUDENTS how the author manages to intensify the feeling of joy and relief on the FOB. *In lines 148–152, the author contrasts the happy sounds of the family members with the information that they have lost their home, and still they are happy. Cummings's commenting quietly adds to the depth of feeling.*

SHORT RESPONSE

Cite Text Evidence Student responses will vary, but students should cite textual evidence to support their positions about the central idea of the selection. Students should:

- explain what the central idea is of the piece.
- give reasons for their point of view.
- cite specific textual evidence to support their reasons.

TO CHALLENGE STUDENTS . . .

For more context and a deeper understanding about American troops in the Iraq war, students can do research online.

ASK STUDENTS what they discovered about some of the difficulties American troops faced in Iraq. *Most of the people did not care who was in control—the insurgents or the coalition forces. They did not help the Americans, who, in Corporal Payne's view, were putting their lives on the line for the benefit of Iraq. Not speaking each other's language could make communication difficult, but Americans and the few Iraqis who joined forces with them managed to overcome that problem.*

DIG DEEPER

With the class, return to Question 10, Reread and Discuss. Have students share the results of their discussion.

ASK STUDENTS whether they were satisfied with the outcome of their small-group discussions. Have each group share what the majority opinion was of the group concerning whether or not Cummings had made the right decision to save Izzy's daughter despite what the rules said. What compelling evidence did the groups cite from the text to support this opinion?

- Encourage students to tell whether there was any convincing textual evidence cited by group members holding the minority opinion. If so, why didn't it sway the group's position?
- Have groups explain how they decided whether or not they had found sufficient evidence to support their opinion. Did everyone in the group agree as to what made the evidence sufficient? How did the group resolve any conflict or difference of opinion?
- After each group has shared the results of its discussion, ask whether another group shared any ideas they wished they had brought to the table.

ASK STUDENTS to return to their Short Response answer and to revise it based on the class discussion.

Acknowledgments

"And of Clay Are We Created" from *The Stories of Eva Luna* by Isabel Allende. Text copyright © 1989 by Isabel Allende. English translation copyright © 1991 by Macmillan Publishing Company. Reprinted by permission of Simon & Schuster, Inc. and Agencia Literaria Carmen Balcells.

Excerpt from *Animals in Translation: Using the Mysteries of Autism to Decode Animal Behavior* by Temple Grandin and Catherine Johnson. Text copyright © 2005 by Temple Grandin and Catherine Johnson. Reprinted by permission of Simon & Schuster, Inc. and Betsy Lerner.

Excerpt from *The Good Soldiers* by David Finkel. Text copyright © 2009 by David Finkel. Reprinted by permission of Farrar Straus and Giroux LLC; The Melanie Jackson Agency, and Atlantic Books.

Excerpt from "Introduction: Love's Vocabulary" from *A Natural History of Love* by Diane Ackerman. Text copyright © 1994 by Diane Ackerman. Reprinted by permission of Random House, Inc. Any third party use of this material, outside of this publication, is prohibited. Interested parties must apply directly to Random House, Inc. for permission.

"Making the Future Better Together" (retitled from "After September 11, 2011, Focus on the Next 10 Years") by Eboo Patel from *The Washington Post,* September 12, 2011. Text copyright © 2011 by Eboo Patel. Reprinted by permission of Eboo Patel.

"Marie Colvin: 'Our mission is to report these horrors of war with accuracy and without prejudice'" by Marie Colvin from *The Guardian,* February 22, 2012, www.guardian.co.uk. Text copyright © by Marie Colvin. Reprinted by permission of the Estate of Marie Colvin.

"My Ceremony for Taking" by Lara Mann from www.drunkenboat.com, November 15, 2012. Text copyright © 2012 by Lara Mann. Reprinted by permission of Drunken Boat.

"Night Calls" by Lisa Fugard from *Outside,* Vol. xx, No. 5, May 1995. Text copyright © 1995 by Lisa Fugard. Reprinted by permission of Lisa Fugard.

Excerpts from *The Odyssey* by Homer, translated by Robert Fitzgerald. Translation copyright © 1961, 1963 by Robert Fitzgerald, renewed © 1989 by Benedict R.C. Fitzgerald on behalf of the Fitzgerald children. Reprinted by permission of Farrar Straus and Giroux LLC and Benedict Fitzgerald.

Excerpt from "Introduction" from *An Ordinary Man: An Autobiography* by Paul Rusesabagina, with Tom Zoellner. Text copyright © 2006 by Paul Rusesabagina. Reprinted by permission of Viking Penguin, a division of Penguin Group (USA) Inc.

"The Prisoner Who Wore Glasses" from *Tales of Tenderness and Power* by Bessie Head. Text copyright © 1989 by The Estate of Bessie Head. Reprinted by permission of Johnson & Alcock.

"The Stayer" from *Palm Crows* by Virgil Suárez. Text copyrights © 2001 by Virgil Suárez. Reprinted by permission of The University of Arizona Press.

"The Survivor" from *The Phoenix Gone, The Terrace Empty* by Marilyn Chin. Text copyright © 1994 by Marilyn Chin. Reproduced with permission of Milkweed Editions.

Excerpt from "What Can I Do to Make Things Better" by Kofi Annan from *Parade Magazine.* Text copyright © by Kofi Annan. Reprinted by permission of Kofi Annan.

"Who Understands Me But Me" from *Immigrants in Our Own Land* by Jimmy Santiago Baca. Text copyright © 1977, 1979, 1981, 1982, 1990 by Jimmy Santiago Baca. Reprinted by permission of New Directions Publishing Corporation.

Index of Titles & Authors